little
BIG LEAGUERS™

By Bruce Nash and Allan Zullo
Compiled by Bernie Ward

LITTLE SIMON
Published by Simon & Schuster Inc., New York

ACKNOWLEDGMENTS

We wish to thank the following players' relatives, friends, former teammates, and coaches for generously helping us obtain childhood photographs: Nancy Sax Aquire, Marvin Arnette, Joe and Joan Benzinger, Barbara Blackman, Win Boggs, Louis and Joan Bosio, Jim Carter, Joe Carter Sr., Kip Dellinger, Don Elster, James Franco, Bill Gaetti, Kent Garrett, Tony Gubicza, Epy Guerrero, Beth Hurst, Claire Kennedy, James Kittle, O.J. Knighten, Jessie Lawson, Wilson Leonard, Frank Marshall, M.H. McGaffigan, Bob and Barbara Moreland, Charles and Betty Murphy, Larry O'Brien, Bill Olson, Charles Pagliarulo, Joe Perruccio, Lefty Renaud, Lettie Reynolds, Vi Ripken, Natalie Senyk, Bette Smemo, Howard Sundberg, Norma Davis Thomas, Marilyn Valle, James Van Slyke, Johnie Wilson, Roland and Donna Worrell, Jessie Wyatt and Bill and Alice Yearout.

We are grateful to the following reporters who contributed valuable player interviews: Bill Althaus, Ann Bauleke, Ron Cook, Paul Hagen, Larry LaRue, Mike Paolercio, Tom Pedulla, Jason Quick, Rob Rains, Larry Schwartz, Melody Simmons, and Casey Tefertiller.

Special thanks go to Tom DiPace for his fine action photos and to Steve Keener of Little League of America for his assistance. We also appreciate the help we received from Julio Mateus and the public relations offices of the major league teams.

PHOTO CREDITS

Tom DiPace—Raines, G. Carter, Marshall, Brett, Gubicza, Murphy, Sax, Boggs, Jackson, J. Carter, Sundberg, Fernandez, Gaetti, Bosio, Van Slyke, Gwynn, Moseby, Ripken, Canseco, Rasmussen, Smith, E. Davis, Benzinger, Butler, McClendon, Reynolds, Leonard, Elster, Valle, Lansford, Franco, Moreland, Sutcliffe; Stephen Goldstein Photography—Worrell; Cleveland Indians—Black, O'Brien; Houston Astros—Wilson, G. Davis; Pittsburgh Pirates—Kipper; Texas Rangers—Ryan; San Diego Padres—Pagliarulo, Hurst; Montreal Expos—McGaffigan; Chicago White Sox—Kittle; Oakland Athletics—S. Davis.

Little Simon
Simon & Schuster Building, Rockefeller Center
1230 Avenue of the Americas, New York, New York 10020

10 9 8 7 6 5 4 3 2 1

ISBN: 0-671-69360-3

♦ ♦ ♦

To Sophie—the wind beneath my wings.
B.N.

To Adam Holt—a little leaguer with
a big league heart.
A.Z.

To my sons Dan and Cody—
They're both major leaguers to me.
B.W.

You probably know a lot about your favorite major league stars by watching them play on television or by reading about them in magazines and in the sports pages. It's likely you know almost everything about them from their batting averages to their ERA's.

But chances are you've read very little, if anything, about the stars' playing days when they were kids. That's what *little BIG LEAGUERS* is all about. Here you will find amazing, never-before-told boyhood stories of today's major leaguers along with previously unseen photos of them playing ball as kids.

The material in this book comes from interviews with superstars, All-Stars, rookies and veterans about their days playing little league or sandlot baseball. About two-thirds of today's major leaguers were once Little Leaguers. When we approached the players, they were delighted to talk about their early days growing up on the baseball diamond. Many of the players revealed their treasured boyhood experiences for the very first time.

Their stories cover a wide range of emotions—some are funny, others are sad; some are zany, others are inspiring. For instance, Pittsburgh Pirates outfielder, Andy Van Slyke, laughed as he recounted the time he wet his pants after making a sensational catch. Talk about embarrassing! Oakland Athletics pitcher Storm Davis recalled the time he was brought in to pitch the last inning with his team ahead 16-0—and lost the game 17-16! Then there are the stories that tug at your heart. New York Yankees second baseman Steve Sax revealed how he promised to hit a home run for his dying father, and then went out and slugged a round-tripper. And we learned that Toronto Blue Jays All-Star shortstop Tony Fernandez was so poor that he used a homemade glove fashioned out of a milk carton and string.

In addition to the players themselves, their parents, former coaches and teammates told their sides of the stories as well. They also helped us obtain photos of these stars as they looked in their little league glory days. These photos accompany the stories in this book and they also appear on the *little BIG LEAGUER* baseball cards in the special bonus section.

Perhaps when you read the book, you'll identify with some of the experiences—both good and bad—that these players had in their youth. Who knows—perhaps one day *your* story will appear in a book about little leaguers who made it to the big leagues.

DALE MURPHY

Outfielder

Atlanta Braves

♦ ♦ ♦

For 8-year-old Dale Murphy, this was the day he had been dreaming about. It was his very first baseball game, and an excited Dale jumped up and down in the dugout.

Not only that, but the coach had just handed him the ball and told him he would be the starting pitcher. It was all too good to be true!

Dale marched proudly out to the mound like a veteran. Out of the corner of his eye, he could see his mom and dad and all his friends watching him as he took his warm-up throws. That just made him more determined to show everybody how good he was.

Dale looked around the field and rubbed up the ball the way he had seen big leaguers do on television. When the umpire yelled, "Play ball!" Dale turned back to the plate and looked right into the eyes of the first batter, Jeff Dunn. He was Dale's best friend!

The pair had grown up in Portland, Oregon, where they did everything together. But when they started little league, they were picked for different teams. It was a big disappointment for both boys. More than anything else, they had wanted to play baseball together.

But now Dale was pitching and Jeff was batting against him. Dale looked in for the sign, went into his windup, threw his very first pitch—and bopped his best friend!

Dale watched in shock as Jeff sat down in the dirt rubbing his shoulder. Jeff wasn't hurt, just surprised that his buddy had plunked him. "It hurt Dale a lot more than it hurt me," Jeff recalled.

In fact, Dale was so embarrassed and afraid over hurting his friend that he ran over to the bench and sat down and cried. Only when the coach convinced him that Jeff was okay did Dale go back to the mound and resume pitching.

That wasn't all that went wrong during Dale Murphy's first year in baseball. It was all so new to him that he didn't even know how to wear a uniform.

"Dale was so excited when he got his first uniform he could hardly wait to try it on," his mother, Betty Murphy, said. "But he really struggled with it. He couldn't figure out how the socks and stirrups worked, so I had to show him how to wear them.

"Dale is a quick learner," she laughed. "I didn't have to show him how after that. But that was his glorious start in baseball as an 8-year-old."

Today, Dale laughs about his "rookie" year jitters and his weak bat. The guy who became the Atlanta Braves' All-Star slugger said he had only *one hit* his entire first season!

"I didn't have the greatest first year a kid ever had," Dale said. "Even though I got just the one hit all year, my folks encouraged me, so I didn't know how bad I was."

No one bawled Dale out at home for not playing well. A lot of kids might have given up if their folks had made fun of them for getting just one hit all year or for hitting their best friend. Dale's parents encouraged him to keep trying and just to have fun playing baseball.

"That's why I have such a positive attitude toward the game today," Dale said.

And that's why the kid whose first year was a dismal failure had the courage to keep trying and improving until he ended up winning the National League's Most Valuable Player award twice.

GEORGE BRETT

The junior varsity coach took one look at the skinny runt trying out for the team and wanted to cut him from the squad.

After all, the ninth grader was only five feet tall. Dripping wet in his baseball warmups, he might have weighed 100 pounds.

But the head coach, John Stevenson, decided to let the kid try out. Stevenson had seen him play as a little leaguer and knew the little guy had talent. By the time he was a senior, George Brett had proved he was a great player. That year he helped win the high school all-star game with his powerful bat. He also pitched in that game, shocking the crowd by mowing down the side, throwing both right- and left-handed!

George grew up in baseball-crazy El Segundo, California, where the whole neighborhood turned out for the games.

A lot of future stars came from that neighborhood. One of them was George's own brother, Ken, who pitched in the World Series in 1967. Scott McGregor, the ace for the Baltimore Orioles, was George's high school teammate.

But George, the skinny little kid who almost got cut, is the one headed for the Baseball Hall of Fame. He demonstrated he was good enough to play in the majors the day he pitched both righty and lefty in his high school all-star game.

In his senior year, George was picked to play in the South Bay All-Star Game. Every year, the top players from 30 high schools were selected for the big game.

George looked like a one-man team. He played shortstop and second base, and scooped up every hot grounder that came his way. He went 2-for-4 at the plate. George also scored once and drove in two runs with a booming home run to lead his East All-Stars to a 6-3 victory.

In the ninth inning, the coach moved

his star infielder to the mound and handed him the ball to pitch.

"George is a real fun-loving guy, and we thought it would be great to show the fans what a tremendous player he was," Coach Stevenson said.

George pitched better than even his coach expected. He struck out the first two batters throwing right-handed, his natural way.

The last man up was a lefty. Suddenly, the coach called time and sent a glove for a left-handed pitcher out to the mound.

"I knew what was going on," George recalled. "I looked over at the dugout and the coach had a funny look in his eye. I knew he was telling me I'd better put that glove on and pitch left-handed.

"I had no idea what was going to happen. I took the glove and switched around to throw left-handed. The batter hit a little dribbler down the third base line. I fielded it and threw him out."

"He didn't just lob it up there either," said Stevenson. "George threw just as hard left-handed as he did right-handed."

Stevenson knew that George was ambidextrous. But the crowd didn't, and when they saw him throwing heat as a southpaw, everyone in the stadium stood up and cheered.

That was George's only official game as a pitcher. But he still likes to surprise his Kansas City Royals teammates by pitching both righty and lefty during batting practice.

The kid who almost didn't make the junior varsity team is the only "switch pitcher" in the big leagues.

STEVE SAX

Steve Sax doesn't hit many home runs. He can remember every one he has hit from the time he started playing as a child.

But there is one homer he remembers most of all. For the All-Star second baseman, it meant more than if he had hit a bases-loaded home run in the bottom of the ninth to win the seventh game of the World Series.

That special home run was the one he promised he would hit for his very sick father.

When Steve and his brother, Dave, were growing up in Sacramento, California, baseball was part of the family. Their dad, John, helped coach. Their mom, Nancy, worked in the concession stand. The boys were such good ballplayers that both of them eventually made it to the major leagues.

Steve says they owe a lot of their success to their dad for his encouragement and coaching. That's why Steve's special home run means so much to him.

When Steve was 16 years old and playing American Legion ball, his dad was very ill with a bad heart. Just before one of Steve's big games, John Sax went into the hospital for open-heart surgery.

On his way to the ballpark, Steve stopped to visit his dad in the hospital. "I told him I was going to hit a home run for him," Steve recalled. "He couldn't talk very well, but he smiled and nodded his head."

It didn't seem possible that Steve could keep his word. That's because the ball-park where the game was played—Clark Field in Woodland, California—had major league dimensions. He had never homered there before, but Steve was determined to make good on his promise.

It didn't take him long. In Steve's first at-bat, he blasted the very first pitch out of the park.

"I didn't hit a lot of home runs as a kid," Steve added. "So when I hit that one and saw it go, I couldn't believe it. That first pitch was the only good one I saw all night and it went way, way out. Left center field."

Steve got the ball back and after the game, he took it to the hospital. He wrote a special message on the ball and put it on a little stand. When his dad came out of surgery, the prized home run ball was at his bedside.

Although Steve went on to become a major league star, he said that nothing tops the home run he hit for his dad. It's still Steve's greatest thrill in baseball.

A few years ago, Steve's dad passed away. He was only 47 years old, but he got to see both of his boys play in the major leagues.

Steve named his own son after his dad. When young John grows up, Steve plans to give him that home run ball with the special message written on it:

"Dad, I kept my promise."

BRUCE HURST

Pitcher
___
San Diego Padres

♦ ♦ ♦

The greatest pitchers in baseball came to St. George, Utah, to teach Bruce Hurst how to throw a slider and a curve ball.

Every week, guys like Tom Seaver, Jim Palmer, Catfish Hunter, and Nolan Ryan showed up with tips on how to make it to the major leagues.

They never came in person. They came in magazines such as *Sports Illustrated* or *Sport* or *The Sporting News*. For Bruce and his coach, Kent Garrett, the pictures in the magazines were almost as good as the real thing.

They helped teach Bruce how to become one of today's top left-handed pitchers.

When Bruce was 13 years old, Kent started coaching him. There weren't any instructional videos on how to pitch and there weren't many games on television

so Kent started using pictures from magazines to teach Bruce some of the basic motions.

"We spent hours cutting out all the pictures of pitchers," Bruce recalled. "We'd study their windups, their arm positions, and how they lifted their knees. We made books of pictures and then we would flip through them and find all the right positions."

Bruce would go to Kent's clothing store to cut out the photographs. They searched for pictures that would show the kind of pitching motion or body position Kent wanted Bruce to learn.

Kent is right-handed and Bruce is left-handed. Kent would stand in front of the store's three-way mirror and go through the motion so Bruce could see how it looked as a left-hander.

Later, Bruce went to the field to practice

what he had studied in the pictures and watched in the mirror.

Kent and Bruce broke the pitching motion down into each stage. They studied how high a pitcher lifted his leg, where he pointed his foot, where he held his hands, and how his foot landed.

"We studied a lot of pictures of Tom Seaver that showed his knee lift because I liked the way he did it," Kent said. "That's why Bruce has such a high knee lift when he pitches today."

Bruce was a good athlete, but his pitching didn't come naturally. In one of his early games, he walked 13 batters. As he studied the photos showing how major leaguers pitched, his control got better and better.

By the time he made it to the majors, Bruce no longer needed to cut out pictures. As a big league starter, he could talk face-to-face with some of the great stars from his books.

In 1986, when Bruce was on the Red Sox pitching staff, one of his teammates in the bullpen was none other than Tom Seaver.

"That was great," Bruce said. "I asked him to show me in person how he did all those things I used to study in his pictures."

JOSE CANSECO

Outfielder

Oakland Athletics

♦ ♦ ♦

Jose Canseco was too excited to eat or sleep. Jose and his brother, Ozzie, had just put on their first little league uniforms. To the 10-year-old twins, those Carol City Chiefs uniforms were more valuable than a World Series ring.

"It was the first time I participated in any team sport and I didn't know anything about organized baseball," recalled Jose, the American League's MVP in 1988. "But I knew that uniform was the most beautiful thing I'd ever seen.

"Like most little league uniforms, it was too big for me, but I was just so happy to be part of a team and have a uniform to put on that I didn't care how it looked."

Jose was so proud of that first uniform that his parents had trouble getting him to change to his regular clothes after base-

ball practice. He wore the red and white Chiefs uniform to meals. Sometimes he even wore it to bed. Jose was ready to wear it to church, but his parents said no.

Jose often wore his new uniform to school in the Miami suburb of Carol City. When the older kids teased him about wearing the uniform all the time, Jose went to school wearing his regular street clothes—*over* his prized uniform!

The only thing Jose loved more than his uniform was playing baseball in it. But when he started in little league, he stood only 4 feet, 4 inches tall. "I was the smallest, the weakest, and the sorriest one out there," Jose said. "I had to struggle just to make the team."

Jose wasn't even a starter most of that first season. So when he won the Most

Valuable Player trophy in the league's all-star game at the end of the season, Jose was as surprised as everyone else. He had to beat out some of the best players in the Miami area to win the award.

"Danny Tartabull [Kansas City Royals] and Rafael Palmeiro [Texas Rangers] were on the same all-star team," Jose said. "They were two years older than I was, and even then, everybody thought those guys were going to the major leagues."

Jose didn't start that all-star game, and played only five innings at third base. But he went 3-for-3, including two singles and a booming double off the Carol City park's "little Green Monster" wall that drove in the game's winning run.

One of the prizes for being named MVP was a new glove. "It probably cost less than $50, but that was awesome in those days," Jose recalled. "Kids would do anything for a glove like that. It was one of the most exciting things that ever happened to me.

"They also gave me a bat and a trophy. I still have that trophy at home. I was just a slow, skinny little kid, but winning that trophy over guys like Danny and Rafael started me thinking that one day I could be a major leaguer."

ERIC DAVIS

Outfielder
Cincinnati
Reds

◆ ◆ ◆

The first time Eric Davis tried out for a little league team, he deliberately hid his enormous talents from the watchful eyes of the league coaches. He dogged it in the field so they wouldn't see how good he really was.

Eric, the Cincinnati Reds' All-Star center fielder, was acting under orders from another coach, O.J. Knighten, who wanted to make sure Eric played for his team.

Although he was barely over four feet tall, Eric was planning on a basketball career when Coach Knighten spotted him dribbling a ball in a neighborhood pick-up game in the Baldwin Hills section of Los Angeles. "I could see the kid had the moves of a great baseball player," Knighten said. "Eric was 11 years old and

had never played baseball, but I wanted him on my team so I hid him from the other coaches. You might say I stole Eric Davis."

When Knighten asked the future major league slugger to try out for a spot on his team, Eric refused. He wanted to devote his time to basketball, even though the other kids towered over him.

"I talked him into trying baseball," Knighten said. "I agreed to pick him up and take him home after the games. That meant a long drive across town, but it was worth it if I could get him on my team."

The six coaches in the Baldwin Hills Baseball Association graded the players during tryouts each year and then held a draft to decide how the teams would be divided up.

"Coach Knighten had watched me hit and field the ball," Eric recalled. "At the tryouts, he told me to act clumsy and look like I couldn't play."

Eric followed Knighten's instructions. He swung at and missed balls he could easily have hit to the wall. He dropped lazy fly balls and booted slow grounders. In a simple game of catch, Eric let the ball slip through his fingers. The other coaches saw exactly what Knighten wanted them to see—an undersized, no-hit, no-field kid who barely knew a baseball from a bat.

Knighten's plan worked. The other coaches didn't draft Eric, but Knighten made him his first-round selection.

It was the first and last time Eric dogged it on the field. Even though his teammates had been playing for six years when he started, Eric, with his raw talent, caught up and surpassed them overnight.

News of Eric's amazing baseball talents spread quickly, and by the end of his second year, he was playing on three different teams.

"I played on one team in the morning, one in the afternoon, and one in the evening," Eric said. "Coaches from other teams came to pick me up and take me to play for them. But no one taught me the fundamentals. I learned everything on my own."

Competing on all those teams gave Eric the extra experience he needed to develop his major league talent. But one former little league teammate, who started playing long before Eric did, made it to the big leagues first.

"He always teased me about that," Eric said. "But now, every time we play the New York Mets, I enjoy reminding Darryl Strawberry that I finally caught up with him."

RICK SUTCLIFFE

Rick Sutcliffe earned money by learning how to pitch. His Grandpa Yearout made him spend 10 minutes every day practicing his pitching motion. Part of the practice involved picking up nickels.

"I don't think Grandpa had played much ball, but he always seemed to know the right thing to do and when to do it," said the 1984 Cy Young winner. "He started working with me when I was about 9 years old. If it wasn't for him, I wouldn't be in the big leagues today."

One of the first things Bill Yearout did was take his young grandson to a pitching clinic put on by the old Kansas City Athletics. One of the tricks they taught him was to pitch from an imaginary "T" on the mound. A pitcher would start his motion from the bottom of the "T". If his follow-through foot came down on either side at the top of the "T," he knew he was off-line and that his motion was wrong.

"Grandpa taped a big 'T' on the basement floor of our home in Independence, Missouri, and put up a full-length mirror so I could watch my own motion," Rick said. "One of the hardest things for anybody to do, especially kids, is throw strikes. The secret is to make the same motion every time. When your body starts doing everything automatically, then you can make adjustments with your hand and arm. Using the 'T' taught me to use the same motion every time I pitched."

Once Rick got the motion down pat, his Grandpa started putting nickels down on the floor beside Rick's foot. If his follow through was on line, Rick could reach down and pick up the nickels and keep them.

"I wasn't very serious about pitching then," Rick remembered. "I did it mainly because I wanted the nickels. Also, I figured that if I couldn't spend 10 minutes a day practicing, then baseball probably wasn't important to me after all."

As he got better, Rick discovered that he had a great curve ball and was anxious to show it off in his little league games. Luckily for Rick, Grandpa Yearout also spotted Rick's curve ball about the time he started throwing it.

"He put a stop to that real fast," Rick said. "If he caught me throwing a curve ball, I got a spanking because I was still too young and could have hurt my arm. I know that's why my arm is so strong today."

When Rick was a senior in high school, his Grandpa decided Rick was ready to uncork his curve ball. He took Rick to another pitching clinic to make sure he learned to throw a curve the right way.

Thanks to his Grandpa, Rick is also known as a pretty good hitter for a pitcher. That's because before every little league game, they went to a batting cage with an automatic pitching machine. His Grandpa fed quarters into the machine and Rick swung away.

"He's still teaching me to hit," Rick said. "I flew home for a visit between games not long ago. I hadn't been hitting too well, so the first thing he did was take me to the batting cage.

"He fed the machine and I got in there and practiced. Just like when I was a kid."

BOB KIPPER

Pitcher
——————
Pittsburgh Pirates

◆ ◆ ◆

"**R**ock and fire, Bobby! Rock and fire!" The catcher crouched behind the homemade plate in the Illinois farm field and yelled encouragement at the kid on the mound. The catcher didn't look like a typical ballplayer. But *she* was the best catcher—and coach—Pirate hurler Bob Kipper ever had.

That catcher was his mom, Wanda, and she's one of the reasons Bob is a big league pitcher today. Starting when he was about 5 years old, his mom was out there behind the plate teaching Bob how to pitch.

Bob, his two brothers, and three sisters grew up on a six-acre farm outside Aurora, Illinois. His dad had to work different shifts away from home, so Wanda and the kids took care of growing the crops and playing baseball.

During the summer, all the kids worked in the fields in the morning and held practice in the afternoon on the one acre the Kippers set aside for ballplaying. After the chores were finished, they grabbed the balls, bats, and gloves. Their mom made a game out of learning the fundamentals. They had contests to see who could go the longest without dropping the ball while warming up.

Then for Bob, it was time to pitch. And that didn't mean just playing more catch. The family had built a pitcher's mound with a pitching rubber and had measured off the regulation distance to home plate. Bob's mom made him throw enough pitches to her every day to add up to a six- or nine-inning game.

"When Bob missed my target and threw a wild pitch, I made him go get the ball himself," his mom recalled. "Sometimes he had to chase the ball so often he would have tears in his eyes. Sooner or later, he had to hit the catcher's mitt. I made him repeat and repeat and repeat until he learned control."

Bob always had a strong arm and, as he got older, he threw harder and harder. By the time he was 14 years old, he was already throwing 80 mph. Finally, his pitches got too hot for his mother to handle. During practice one day, he reared back and let one fly.

"His pitch ripped the webbing right out of my glove," his mom said. "That's when I knew it was time to turn the catching over to his older brother Dan."

The most important thing Bob's mom taught him about pitching was to get the proper rhythm. Rock and fire.

"It's hard for a kid to understand what you mean by the mechanics of pitching," Bob said. "Now I understand what that means. Even today when I'm pitching and get in a jam, I'll think about what Mom used to tell me about finding the rhythm and that settles me down."

Bob Kipper may be out there on the mound in a big league park, but he can still hear his mom yelling: "Rock and fire, Bobby! Rock and fire!"

LLOYD McCLENDON

Infielder-Outfielder

Chicago Cubs

◆ ◆ ◆

Lloyd McClendon swung his bat only five times in the 1971 Little League World Series, but those five swings put him in the record book as one of the greatest players in the history of the Series.

They called the 12-year-old Lloyd the "new Sultan of Swat"—named after famed slugger Babe Ruth—when Lloyd belted five home runs in five consecutive official plate appearances. He might have hit 10 round-trippers, but he was intentionally walked the five other times he went to bat.

"It was the impossible dream coming true right before our eyes," Lloyd's coach, Jessie Lawson, recalled. "We knew how good Lloyd was, but he showed the rest of the world he was probably the greatest Little League player of all time."

Lloyd's awesome performance wasn't just with the bat. During the three-game World Series, he also pitched two of the games, winning one of them.

Lloyd was the main reason his Gary, Indiana, Little League team made it all the way to the World Series. He excelled as a pitcher and catcher, but it was his booming bat all season long that carried the team to the championships.

His team's first opponent in the Series was from Lexington, Kentucky. Lloyd pitched and won the game, 7 - 2. The first time he came to bat in the game, Lloyd hit the first pitch thrown to him out of the park. His second home run came in the third inning—again on the first pitch.

The third time up, Lloyd was walked intentionally. But he had already driven in four of his team's seven runs.

In the second game against a team from Madrid, Spain, Lloyd caught and repeated his home run show. His first inning homer drove in two runs and tied a record for three home runs in one World Series.

On his next trip to the plate—and with his fourth swing of the bat—Lloyd belted another dinger and shattered the old record. His fourth World Series home run powered his team to a 7 - 0 victory over Spain.

"We had a pretty good idea what would happen the next time Lloyd came up," Coach Lawson said. "They walked him again."

The championship game was against Tainan, Taiwan, and Lloyd knew it would be the toughest game of his young career. Tainan was going for its second World Series title in three years and Lloyd had to come back to pitch with only one day's rest.

It was a spectacular finish, even though Lloyd's team lost.

A single and a walk put two Gary runners on base in the first inning. When Lloyd came to bat, the crowd of 30,000 fans gave him a standing ovation. And, as if on cue, he drove the first pitch thrown to him out of the park. It was an incredible feat: Five swings. Five home runs.

Tainan picked up one run in the third inning and two in the fourth to tie the game. But Lloyd never got another chance to add to his amazing home run total. He was intentionally walked three more times as the game went beyond the regulation six innings. In the ninth inning, Tainan came alive and scored nine runs to win the Series.

But who won that Little League World Series wasn't nearly as memorable as what Lloyd McClendon did there. It will always be remembered as the Series when Lloyd became a Little League legend with his five home runs on five swings of the bat.

DAVE VALLE

Catcher
———
Seattle
Mariners

◆ ◆ ◆

Dave Valle wore a mask to play base-ball long before he ever donned his catcher's gear and went behind the plate. During the first year Dave played in little league, his father made him wear a hockey mask when he went to bat.

"My father signed me up to play in the 8-year-old league when I was only 6," Dave recalled. "He was worried about my reaction time against those older pitchers. He bought a hockey mask and said I had to wear it.

"I fought against wearing it, but he wouldn't give in. He said that if I didn't wear the mask, I couldn't play baseball. I really wanted to play, so that ended the argument," recalled the Seattle Mariners' defensive standout behind the plate.

Dave got his early start playing in "Chicken Coop Stadium"—a batting cage his father, John, built out of old boards and chicken wire. "We had this batting cage in our backyard right in the middle of New York City," Dave said. "It became the focal point for the kids in the neighborhood, and all the little leaguers my father coached came there to practice. We even had a little Iron Mike pitching machine which used tennis balls instead of baseballs."

John Valle spotted his son's talents there in "Chicken Coop Stadium" long before Dave was big enough to play for his father's little league team. But by the time Dave was 6 years old, his dad felt he was ready to compete—as long as he wore the hockey mask.

"I had to wear it every time I batted that

first year," Dave said. "I hated it. It was hot and uncomfortable and the other kids really rode me pretty hard about it. Kids can really get on someone who is a little different, and wearing a hockey mask to bat in little league games definitely made me stand out."

Dave said he never got hit in the face while he wore the mask. After several games, he was so used to wearing it that it became like a security blanket for him. He felt that as long as he had the mask on, he couldn't get hurt. The mask helped him develop his confidence at the plate.

"I think my dad had me wear the mask as much for my psychological protection as for my physical protection," Dave recalled. "I was a little afraid of those older guys at first. Some of them looked like giants on the mound. When I finally did stop wearing the mask, it took me a while to get used to hitting without it."

The first time Dave went to bat in his second year of little league, he put the mask on out of habit. But his father told him to take it off. Dave didn't have to wear it anymore because he was a good enough hitter. His dad said that Dave was now ready to hit against the best pitchers in his little league.

"When my dad told me that I didn't have to wear the mask, it was like a coming of age. I felt like I had proven myself in his eyes. It was probably my proudest moment as a kid."

TONY FERNANDEZ

Infielder
___
Toronto
Blue
Jays

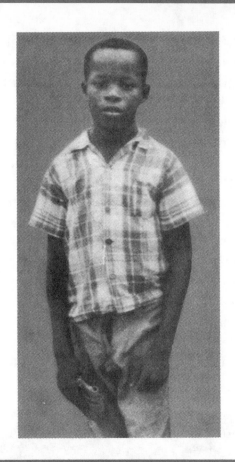

When Toronto Blue Jays' scout Epy Guerrero took a second look at the kid trying out for shortstop, he couldn't believe his eyes. The youngster snared every grounder hit his way. But what was more amazing was that the kid didn't even have a regular leather glove. Instead, he used a homemade glove—one fashioned from an old milk carton and pieces of string!

Tony Fernandez wasn't much different from all the other baseball-crazy kids in the Dominican Republic. He had his heart set on playing baseball in the major leagues and he was willing to do anything to get the chance.

Everything was against Tony—no uniform, no shoes, no glove. He lived with his 10 brothers and sisters in San Pedro de Macoris, one of the poorest villages in the country. The family's home was a shack behind the center field fence at San Pedro's Tetelo Vargas Stadium. Whenever Epy came to town to hold tryouts for older players, Tony would scramble over the fence all ready to play.

Tony knew that one day he could be the Gold Glove, All-Star shortstop that he is today. Back then, he didn't need shoes or even a glove to prove it. Because he grew up in a poor family, Tony had to do without a lot of things. He had to make his own baseball equipment because his family couldn't afford to buy it.

Any kid can play barefooted, even on San Pedro's rocky, uneven fields. However, being without a glove was something else. But that didn't stop Tony. He rummaged around in the trash pile and found an old milk carton. He cut it into the shape of a glove and tied it to his hand with pieces of string.

One day, when Epy came to town again, Tony stood out at shortstop with his milk carton glove, begging for a chance to show off his fielding skills. Just give him the opportunity to make it to the *gran carpa*, the big leagues.

Epy gave Tony that chance. He knew that some of the best players in baseball came from this remote little village. Maybe Tony would be another George Bell, Damaso Garcia, Mariano Duncan, Rafael Ramirez, or Stan Javier.

But none of them had more desire than the kid with the milk carton glove. When Epy couldn't take his pestering anymore, he started hitting hard grounders to Tony. The kid was like a vacuum cleaner at shortstop. He scooped up ground balls as fast as Epy could hit them.

"Tony was amazing," Epy said. "All he had was that old milk carton glove, but he could stop anything I hit to him. You'd think he had the most expensive glove in the world."

When Epy got too tired to hit any more, he had two former major league stars, Rico Carty and Manny Mota, help him. The two took turns hitting balls to Tony as hard as they could.

"Not very many got by him," Epy remembered. "I told him that someday he would play in the majors. I knew he could be the best shortstop in baseball."

With Epy's help, Tony got his chance to play. He traded in his milk carton glove for the real thing and signed with the Toronto Blue Jays.

Today, he plays with the best glove money can buy. The Canadian fans love him, but nowhere is he a bigger hero than in San Pedro de Macoris. A lot of kids there can't afford baseball gloves or shoes, but they believe that if Tony Fernandez could start out with just a milk carton for a glove and make it all the way to the *gran carpa*, maybe they can, too.

OZZIE SMITH

Infielder
***
St. Louis Cardinals

♦ ♦ ♦

As a lonely, little boy growing up in Mobile, Alabama, and later in Los Angeles, California, a baseball was Ozzie Smith's best friend. His older brothers often left him to play alone, so Ozzie had to create his own games and sometimes even his own playmates. "Like any other best friend, we went everywhere and did everything together. My best friend helped me make it to the major leagues," recalled Ozzie.

The games he invented to play with his best friend were the kind that turned Ozzie into a quick-footed All-Star short-stop with a strong, accurate arm and lightning-fast reflexes.

Ozzie called one of his games "wall ball." He made a mark on the side of a building and then practiced for hours throwing the ball at the spot. He used a rubber ball that bounced back to him, so by fielding the ball after he threw it, Ozzie also was developing the skills that have made him a sure-handed National League shortstop today.

Sometimes Ozzie stood with his back to the wall, then whirled and threw the ball at the spot. This exercise improved his quickness and throwing accuracy. Those talents now make him one of the best in baseball at turning a double play.

When he wasn't throwing at the wall, Ozzie threw at the steps in front of his house. He tried to anticipate how the ball would bounce so he could be in the right spot to catch the carom. Today, whenever

Ozzie plays on a rough infield where the ball takes crazy bounces, he remembers that early game that taught him to anticipate the ball.

"Another thing I'd do was lay on my back, close my eyes, throw the ball straight up in the air and try to catch it when it came down," Ozzie said. "That helped me develop a feel for where the ball would be."

Ozzie played a variation of that game outdoors at twilight time just after the street lights came on. He threw the ball as high as he could into the darkness and caught it as it came down through the glow of the street lights.

"I didn't think about it at the time, but those two games enhanced my concentration and my hand-eye coordination," Ozzie said. "Those are skills that every major leaguer has to have."

But of all the games Ozzie played with his best friend, his favorite was "over the house." His house had a slanted roof. Ozzie would throw the ball over the roof, run around the house, and try to catch the ball before it rolled off on the other side.

"I didn't catch it, but I came close," Ozzie recalled. "That game built up my speed. But I made it more than just an exercise. I'd pretend that I was running in the outfield to make the game-saving catch in the World Series. I was going to get around the house and make that catch no matter what, but I never did.

"I gained something more valuable than speed from that game. I learned desire and determination."

PETE O'BRIEN

Infielder

Cleveland Indians

◆ ◆ ◆

Ten-year-old Pete O'Brien pounded an old tire with his bat until his hands were raw. He climbed a rope to build up his strength. And he hit against 20-year-olds who threw tennis balls at him as hard as they could—from only 30 feet away.

The unusual training methods for the Cleveland Indians' power hitter started when he was only 5 years old. Little League coach Danny Petta believed that even young players could benefit from conditioning and strength training. Danny hung a couple of ropes from a tree in his back yard. Every morning and every evening, Pete went to Danny's yard and worked out. He had to climb one rope over and over again to build up his upper body strength.

At the end of the second rope, Danny had tied an old rubber tire. Pete used the tire for batting practice. For hours, he pounded away at the tire with his bat. The resistance that came from hitting the tire helped build up the strength in his forearms. Sometimes, Pete swung at the tire until his hands bled. But he feels it was worth it. Today, he's known as one of the most powerful sluggers in the majors.

That training came in handy years before Pete reached the major leagues. When he was 10 years old, he started competing in pickup games against players twice his age.

With four older brothers, there was always a gang hanging out around Pete's house in Santa Monica, California. Most of them, like his brother, Larry, were 10 years older than Pete. A few were even playing baseball in college. Pete loved to tag along when they all trooped down to the diamond at Roosevelt Elementary School for a game.

"Pete was welcome, but the deal was that if he got hurt or cried, he had to go home," Larry recalled. "He did okay. After about a year, some of my friends were picking him to be on their teams."

Pete was rarely sent home. Instead, being forced to keep up with that tough competition at an early age helped prepare him for the big leagues He started developing his quick reflexes at the plate during tennis ball games in the O'Brien's driveway.

During those games, the batter stood with his back to the garage door. The pitcher was less than 30 feet away. No one took it easy with Pete just because he was a kid. They still threw as hard as they could. But Pete seldom struck out and never backed down. "He developed his good hitting eye and quick bat just trying to keep up with us," Larry said. "Pete was really a tough kid."

"I still use some of those drills, like hitting the tire," Pete said. "The first time I knew the drills were making me a stronger hitter was when I was in Little League. The other team was trying to walk me intentionally. I didn't like it, so I just reached out and swatted a double to left field. It surprised everybody—including me."

TONY GWYNN

Outfielder

San Diego Padres

◆ ◆ ◆

When the Long Beach Cubs played an away game, they never felt that the other team had the home field advantage. That's because Tony Gwynn and his teammates climbed over fences to practice on their opponents' fields before every big game.

"We'd go around to wherever the game was to be played, sneak in, and practice on the field the day before the game," recalled the National League's three-time batting champion. "Most of the time, nobody knew we were there."

The idea for practicing on the other team's field came from the Cubs' coach, Joe Perruccio. He started coaching Tony when the future All-Star player went out for organized baseball for the first time at the age of 11.

"We traveled all over Southern California for our special practices," Joe said. "Some fields were grass, and others were all dirt. I wanted the kids to be familiar with the field they had to play on so there wouldn't be any surprises when the game started.

"The other teams may have thought they had the home field advantage, but they never knew about our 'practice raids.'"

One championship game was scheduled at a community college. When the Cubs arrived early for practice, they found the field surrounded by a high fence and the gates locked. "That didn't stop us," Joe said. "Tony was the first over the 15-foot high fence and the rest of us followed him—the team, the coach, and the equipment bag. It wasn't the only fence we climbed over for a secret practice, but it was the highest."

The Cubs' plan seldom failed. The team rarely lost. And it wasn't unusual for Tony and his teammates to pile up such lopsided scores as 40-0. When the Cubs pulled far ahead of the other team, Joe often made his players turn around and hit from the opposite side of the plate to make the game more even.

But Tony, a natural left-hander, hated to bat from the right side. "It was the only time in my career I had to switch hit, and I didn't like it," Tony said. "I wanted to swing away all the time."

One time, the Cubs had a big lead and the game was running long. Joe Perruccio had tickets for the team to attend the Los Angeles Dodgers' 1,000th game, and it was getting close to game time. "I told the guys to bat the other way so we could get out of there sooner," Joe said. "Tony refused. He loved baseball so much he wanted to keep playing himself instead of going to watch somebody else, even if it was a special Dodger game.

"It's that kind of competitive spirit that makes him a major league batting champion today."

GARY CARTER

For 12-year-old Gary Carter, the 1966 baseball season was just about the best and the worst a kid could have.

That was the year Gary hit a monster home run that had everyone in his hometown of Fullerton, California, talking about the little league kid with the big league power. Along with his thundering bat, Gary also pitched 13 victories without a loss to lead his team to a 20-1 record and the city championship finals.

It was also the season his mother died.

For Gary and his big brother, Gordon, the loss of their mother, Inge, was a terrible blow. She was only 37 years old when she died of leukemia.

"Mom was always there supporting me, encouraging me to do well in sports," said the Mets' captain and 11-time All-Star catcher. "I realize now that she was one of my strengths as a kid."

Even as she grew sicker and sicker, Gary's mom was still there in the stands at every game, urging him on toward his superstar dreams.

Back then, Gary's tremendous talent was obvious. When he wasn't pitching, he was gobbling up grounders at shortstop and driving in runs with his powerful bat. Gary often knocked balls over the little league fence which was 200 feet from home plate.

But it was his 350-foot homer that Fullerton fans will never forget. He walloped it during a game when he was mad at himself. "In my previous at-bat, I struck out—the only time I did that all season," Gary recalled. "This time I wasn't going to let it happen again."

The ball Gary hit soared over the left center field fence at Nicholas Junior High and kept on going. It cleared the street behind the field, sailed over the parking lot at Bob Jones Toyota, and crashed through a window of the auto dealer's showroom.

"From then on," said Jim Carter, Gary's father and coach, "people knew that Gary had the makings of a major leaguer."

As great as it was, that home run would have meant a whole lot more to young Gary if his mom had been there to see it. But Inge Carter had died a few months earlier.

Gary's team was scheduled to play on the day of her funeral, but league officials postponed the game for two days. Everyone would have understood if Gary had decided not to play. But he suited up. "I wanted to play," Gary said. "I knew that's what my mom would have wanted me to do. So I dedicated the game to her."

His father remembered how painful it was for Gary to go out and play. "He loved his mom dearly and really wanted to win that game for her," said Jim Carter.

With his heart still hurting from the loss of his mother, 12-year-old Gary Carter bravely went out to the mound—and pitched a no-hitter! Tears trickled down his face as he proudly walked off the mound with the cheers of teammates and fans ringing in his ears.

Gary ran over to his dad and said, "I sure wish Mom could have been here to see that." Jim Carter put his arm around his son's shoulder and told him, "Gary, you can be sure she's looking down from heaven right now."

Today, whenever Gary Carter appears at baseball card shows and signs autographs for a fee, all that money is donated to the Leukemia Society of America for research. So far, he has raised more than $1 million to help others fight the deadly disease.

And he does it for his mom.

RON KITTLE

Outfielder
—————
Chicago White Sox

◆ ◆ ◆

Ron Kittle's career as a manager was the shortest on record. He lasted two innings. And then his dad arrived at the game—and fired him!

When Ron was 11 years old, his dad, Jim, was managing and coaching the little league team Ron played for in Aetna, Indiana. Jim Kittle was working a lot of overtime that summer and couldn't always be at the field exactly when the game started.

One night he made out the lineup card and gave it to Ron to take to the game with instructions to start the game without him. Ron was the team's star catcher and sometimes played first base. But for this one game, he saw the perfect opportunity to play manager and be the guy who ran the team.

Before the game started, Ron rewrote the whole lineup. He moved his teammates around to different positions. He told them when to bat and how to play. And Ron did something he'd always wanted to do. He pencilled himself in as starting pitcher.

Unfortunately, Ron was a much better catcher than he was a pitcher. He couldn't find the strike zone.

When Jim Kittle arrived, the game was in the second inning and the other team was happily running up the score.

"There was Ron on the mound and a baserunner walking home from third," Jim said. "Another was walking down to first and the bases were still loaded."

Ron's dad took a look at the scoreboard and discovered that the opposing team had already scored a bunch of runs in the first inning, mainly on walks Ron had given up.

Jim Kittle called timeout and strode to the mound. He didn't have to say a word. He just pointed to the bench and brought Ron's brief managing—and pitching—career to a screeching halt.

"Ron just wanted to run things and try his hand at pitching," his dad said. "He knew I wouldn't be around to say no. But he found out real fast that the manager is in charge of the team even if he comes late. Ron knew just as soon as he saw me walk out on the field that he had made a bad move. He didn't even ask to go for ice cream after the game. He just went straight to bed without a word."

That turned out to be the first and only game Ron ever pitched. It was also the first and only little league game in which he was benched. And it was the first and only game that Ron Kittle ever managed.

"I have a lot of good memories about little league, but that definitely was one of my worst experiences," Ron said.

MIKE MARSHALL

As a kid, Dodger right fielder Mike Marshall developed his powerful arm throwing bats and helmets.

Mike didn't lose many games as a little leaguer, but he lost his temper a lot. And it almost cost him a shot at the major leagues and a World Series championship ring.

"I probably got kicked out of more games as a little leaguer than I have since I've been in the majors," recalled the Los Angeles Dodgers' slugger. "No one hated to lose a game more than I did. Now I've got a reputation for being a pretty calm guy who never argues with the umpires. But I wasn't always that way."

His dad, Frank Marshall, was also his coach during Mike's early years in baseball in Buffalo Grove, Illinois. Even he had a hard time keeping the hot-tempered youngster from blowing up over a called strike or an error in the field.

The umpires were always warning Frank to keep Mike away from them. By the time Mike was 12, he was already almost six feet tall and as big as most of the umpires. None of them wanted to tangle with the hot-headed kid.

No one lets Mike forget one of his early blowups. After striking out, he stomped away from the plate, jerked off his helmet, and sent it flying clear over the dugout and into the parking lot.

Andy Farrissey played against Mike all through little league although they were best friends.

"I remember that game," Andy said. "He really let that helmet fly, clean out of sight. We knew how bad his temper was, so we always got on him hard. When he got mad, he didn't play as well.

"One time, we gave him an intentional walk. He started screaming that it wasn't fair that he didn't get a chance to hit. We were laughing at him. That really teed him off and he threw his bat at our coach."

Thanks to some tough words from Andy and a couple of other friends, Mike realized he would have to control his temper. He finally learned his lesson in high school.

His friends had come to watch him play an important high school game between top rivals Buffalo Grove and Arlington High in Illinois. Mike's reputation as a potentially great player had grown and several big league scouts were at the game to look him over.

In the first inning, Mike lost his temper after he drew a walk. He trotted down to first base and deliberately knocked the first baseman down.

"He didn't have to do it," Andy recalled. "He was just mad. He got kicked out of the game and it was only the first inning. Afterwards, we really got on him. We told him there were scouts there and that with his temper he had a good chance of never making it to the big leagues."

Almost overnight, Mike began to change.

"If I hadn't learned to control my temper then, I'm not sure I would have made it to the World Series," Mike reflected. "Kids need to have that fiery competitive spirit, because without it they'll never make it to the majors. But I learned you have to use it playing baseball and not waste it throwing temper tantrums."

NOLAN RYAN

Pitcher
—
Texas
Rangers

◆ ◆ ◆

Eleven-year-old Nolan Ryan was on the mound gunning for a no-hitter. It was another one of those hard-fought pitching duels with Nolan and the opposing pitcher matching strike for strike and out for out. Neither one was giving an inch.

"I didn't even realize until late in the game that I had a no-hitter going," recalled the only pitcher in major league history to record five career no-hitters. "I thought that was really great, but then somebody said the other pitcher also had a no-hitter working and that's when I started worrying. I was more concerned about us winning the game than I was about getting a no-hitter."

The place was Alvin, Texas. The time was summer, 1958. The game pitted the Little League Alvin Rangers against the Alvin Lions. But this wasn't just a routine Little League game. It wasn't even a routine no-hitter that was unfolding. This was a *double* no-hitter in the works.

Nolan was trying to win the first no-hitter of his baseball career. And he was pitching against one of his best friends,

Joe Godwin, who also had his heart set on winning a no-hitter for his team, the Lions.

"We really went at it hard all afternoon," Nolan recalled. "Joe and I had grown up together, but when we were out there playing baseball, each of us wanted to beat the other bad."

The two youngsters battled back and forth. As soon as Nolan set down the side, Joe went to the mound and retired the Rangers the same way. But in the final inning, Joe was the first to crack. He gave up a couple of walks, and then an error in the field loaded the bases.

The Rangers won the game when Joe walked the next batter and forced in the winning run. The final score was 1-0 and Nolan Ryan had pitched his first no-hitter.

"That was the farthest thing from my mind when I went out to pitch that day," Nolan said. "But that game really started me thinking about going to the major leagues. Until then, it was just a fantasy like it is with every other Little Leaguer. The funny thing is, I didn't pitch another no-hitter until I got to high school. And I didn't pitch one in professional baseball until I got to the major leagues.

"But that no-hitter when I was 11 years old still stands out. You never forget the first one."

KEVIN ELSTER

In his first year in organized baseball, Kevin Elster refused to play, so his dad literally had to drag him in tears to the ballpark.

When Kevin, the Mets' defensive stand-out at shortstop, was 4 years old, he already had a mind of his own. One thing he knew for sure was that he didn't like baseball and nobody was going to make him play. When it came time for his dad to take Kevin to sign up, Kevin dug his heels in and refused to go.

"My older brothers all played baseball," Kevin recalled. "My dad took me with them to the playground when they had a game. I had played a lot with my family, so it wasn't that baseball was new to me. I just didn't want to sign up for a team and play."

Don Elster, Kevin's father, had watched the youngster hit and throw the ball around the family's home in Huntington Beach, California. He knew Kevin had excellent hand-eye coordination and that, with the right opportunity, he might grow into a good ball player.

"I didn't think about him being a major leaguer then," Don Elster said. "But I could see he had the raw talent that could develop if he was in the right situation."

The first opportunity was the opening of five-pitch season. Five-pitch was a favorite game where Kevin grew up. Like T-ball, its purpose was to give kids who were too young for Little League a head start in baseball. A softball was used in place of a hard ball. An adult pitched underhanded to the kids, and each batter had five swings before he was out.

"My dad was going to take me down and sign me up," Kevin said. "But I didn't want to play. He literally had to drag me to the car. I was crying all the time, but I didn't get my way.

"I don't recall ever striking out after I finally agreed to play. The first game, I went 5 for 5 and I remember thinking: 'Hey! This is pretty easy after all.'"

Even though most of the other five-pitch players were a year or two older than Kevin, he soon was recognized as the best player in the league. His father didn't have to drag him to the car again, since Kevin now was eager to get in the game and be the star.

But at the end of the season, when players were picked for the all-star game, Kevin was not allowed to play. Officials decided that even though Kevin had been the outstanding player during the regular season, 4 years old was too young to play in the all-star game.

He was banned from the team, and Kevin ended the season the same way he started—in tears.

Infielder
___
Minnesota Twins

◆ ◆ ◆

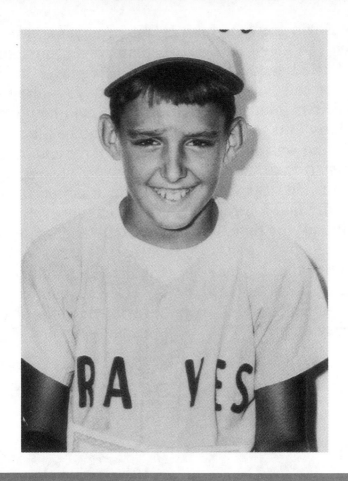

By the time Gary Gaetti was 10 years old, he had played on a team that was so good, the only way to stop it from winning was to break it up and scatter the players.

Gary was the sparkplug of the Central Braves which never lost a game from 1967 through 1969. They won an amazing 50 straight games.

But the Braves were too good for their own good. When the players reached Little League age, league officials decided they didn't want the same team winning all the time. They held a special draft that sent the Braves players to different teams.

"There's no telling how many games we might have won if they had let us stay together," recalled the Minnesota Twins' Gold Glove third baseman. "It didn't seem fair, breaking us up just because we were so good."

After defeating every other team in the Atom League (for kids ages 7 through 9) in Centralia, Illinois, the Braves went on the road. They kept the streak alive by beating other teams throughout southern Illinois. Sometimes the Braves had to drive 60 miles or more to find a team that would play them.

The Braves always won by lopsided scores—17-0, 16-2, 24-0. Only four teams scored against them in all 50 games. Before long, their string of victories was making headlines throughout southern Illinois, and it got harder for them to find a team to play them.

"We had to travel all over that part of the state to find games," Gary's dad, Bill

Gaetti, said. "The 14 regular season games weren't enough for those kids. They begged us parents to find them more baseball games."

Bill Gaetti said that the Braves developed into such a good team because they all grew up playing together. Eight of them lived on the same block.

When the Braves didn't have a regular practice or game, they met at the ball field and invented baseball games of their own. One game they made up was called backwards ball. The Braves used second base as home plate. From there, they could swat short home runs over the regular backstop and pretend they were the St. Louis Cardinals winning the World Series.

During the streak, Gary batted over .400. He also pitched and won 28 games.

When the Braves had won about 40 games, there was a lot of pressure to keep the streak alive. To help the team, Gary learned how to throw a curve ball.

In their final championship game, Gary pitched and struck out 14 batters with his newly developed curve ball. But he paid for it. "I could hardly lift my arm for a couple of days afterwards," he said. "It was a dumb thing to do. I might have hurt my arm and never made it to the majors."

Even though he was the star of the team, Gary said his fondest memories are of the team effort that made the winning streak possible.

"We had a great team because we knew each other so well and had played together so long," Gary added. "Teamwork. That's how we won 50 games. And that's how I've tried to play ever since."

BO JACKSON

Outfielder

Kansas City Royals

◆ ◆ ◆

Bo Jackson had to grow up before he was allowed to play baseball with kids his own age. It wasn't because he was too small or too poor a player. Just the opposite. Bo was too good.

His little league career lasted only a few weeks. Then, while most of his friends were just learning how to hit and throw, Bo was catching for some adult teams.

He was 9 years old when he tried out for baseball. All his friends wanted to be either the pitcher or the first baseman. Nobody wanted to catch, but Bo told the coach he would. He liked the looks of all that gear the catcher wore. And most of all, he liked being behind the plate where all the action was.

"Two weeks later, they told me I couldn't catch anymore in the little league because I was too rough. I wasn't mean. I was just a lot bigger and better than the other guys," recalled the Kansas City Royals' exciting power hitter.

"They moved me up to the Pony League [for kids ages 13 to 15]. I caught with that team for about a month. Then one of my older brothers asked me to catch for his team on Sundays and that was the end of the Pony League."

Bo's reputation as an amazing player spread fast. People came just to see this kid perform his favorite feat—he could throw a ball from home plate to second base while on his knees!

Several of the other small towns around McCullum, Alabama, where Bo grew up had industrial league teams. The players were young adults from 18 to 20 years old, hoping to make it to the majors. The coach of his brothers' team was so impressed with Bo that he soon became the starting catcher.

"I went from little league to catching for industrial league all in one summer," he said. "By the time I was 12 years old, I was playing with men's teams all the time. I never played with guys my own age until I got to junior high school."

Bo loved the excitement he created. When his team traveled to other towns, people laughed and yelled at his manager to get that "baby" off the field before he got hurt.

But when the game started, Bo would scoop balls out of the dirt, pick off runners, and gun down anyone who tried to steal.

"I was best known for my arm," Bo said. "That's because when I was a kid, I didn't do anything except throw rocks. I'd throw rocks day in and day out.

"By the time I was playing in the industrial league, I was famous for throwing guys out from my knees. I'd let them steal second base on purpose and then catch them trying to steal third. They'd go back to the bench shaking their heads and saying, 'That kid never got off his knees!'"

STORM DAVIS

Pitcher
___
Oakland Athletics

◆ ◆ ◆

Storm Davis always wanted to pitch. He finally got his chance when he strode to the mound with his team leading 16-0 in the last inning. All he had to do was get the last three outs for his team to win. He got those last three outs—but only after he gave up 17 runs and lost the game.

"I've heard of guys blowing games, but this was ridiculous," recalled Storm, whose strong pitching helped lead the Oakland A's to the 1988 American League pennant.

Every year, the big rivalry in Jacksonville, Florida little league was between the South Side Twins and the Pine Forest Vikings. Even before Storm started playing for the Twins, the two teams fought tooth and nail with the winner usually going on to the league playoffs.

Storm's dad, George Davis, was coaching the Twins in the summer of 1969 and put Storm, then 7 years old, in right field. But Storm wanted to be a pitcher. He worked on his pitching with his dad in the backyard and Storm was dying to show what he could do on the mound.

Finally, in the biggest game of all, he got his chance against the hated Vikings.

"The game with the Vikings was always a biggie," Storm said. "There was a lot of pride involved in winning that game. If we beat the Vikings, we felt like we'd had a great year."

With a 16-0 lead, it looked like the Twins had this game and bragging rights for the year locked up. Even the Vikings were packing up to go home with their tails between their legs.

Storm had been hanging around in right field with nothing to do the whole game. The Vikings weren't getting any hits and Storm was bored waiting for the game to end so the Twins could start celebrating. He started to trot out to right for the last inning, but his dad stopped him. "We have a pretty big pad," he told Storm. "You go in and finish pitching."

Storm was overjoyed. He'd been begging to try out some of the stuff he'd been working on in the back yard.

"We didn't have anybody left to pitch, but my dad figured with a lead that big, I couldn't do much damage," Storm said. "Was he in for a surprise! Everything that could go wrong did go wrong."

The disaster started when Storm gave up a couple of hits. Then he walked two, before a few errors in the field brought the Vikings roaring back to life.

The runs piled up. The Vikings hit everything Storm threw at them. If they didn't get hits, Storm walked them. The bases filled up as one gleeful Viking after another trotted home with another run.

"I looked over at my dad and all he could do was shrug his shoulders," Storm recalled. "Somehow we finally got three outs, but it was too late. In my first game as a pitcher I had lost a 16-run lead in one inning! It was a nightmare!"

Instead of the Vikings, it was the Twins who went home as losers. But Storm vowed he would wipe out his embarrassing debut. He worked on his control all winter long. When the Twins and the Vikings met again the next year, Storm was the starting pitcher.

His revenge was sweet. He pitched a no-hitter!

JOHN FRANCO

Pitcher
***
Cincinnati Reds

◆ ◆ ◆

John Franco was heartbroken. All of his buddies were running out onto the field for the first day of spring practice. But John had to stand on the sidelines and watch with tears in his eyes. The freshman coach at Lafayette High School in Brooklyn had taken one look at the scrawny little kid and laughed him off the field.

"Come back when you've grown up," he snorted.

John had heard those insults all his life. It was tough always to be the smallest guy on the field. It was even harder if you came from the toughest part of Brooklyn and you had to prove how good you were all the time.

But when tryouts for the freshman squad were held, John didn't even get the chance to show his talent. What made it worse was that he knew he was better than many of the other guys out there.

"I knew I was at least as good as they were," recalled John, one of the National League's top relief pitchers. "I had been playing against them every summer since we were in little league. But I wasn't even 5 feet 5 inches tall then and I weighed less than a hundred pounds. The coach took one look at me and laughed."

John knew he had the strongest arm in Brooklyn and he felt he was being cheated. "I couldn't see where it made any difference if the guy throwing a 90 mph fast ball was five feet tall or six feet tall," he said.

John believed that he was destined to inherit the mound at Lafayette High. It was here where the great Dodger pitcher, Sandy Koufax, had started his ballplaying career and John was determined to follow in his hero's footsteps.

John was bitter about not getting a fair chance. But being laughed off the field because he was undersized was nothing new. His first little league uniform was so big no one could see the number when he tucked in his shirt. As a result, the players, coaches, and parents from the other teams constantly made fun of him.

"They were always yelling about that 'midget' out on the mound and were laughing at me," John recalled. "People in Brooklyn can really be tough when it comes to baseball."

Everyone he played against was bigger and stronger than he was. But John had something they didn't have. He had a can-non for an arm. No kid in Brooklyn could throw as hard as John Franco.

By the next year, John had grown a little and was ready to try again. No one was going to keep him off the mound that belonged to him and Sandy!

With a new coach running things, John got his chance. He easily made the varsity squad and quickly made up for lost time. Before long, he was known as the best high school pitcher in the New York area.

When the major league scouts came around to look him over, John signed with Sandy Koufax's team, the Dodgers. Later, John went to Cincinnati where the littlest guy in Brooklyn little league proved he could play with the big guys—by winning the National League's Fireman of the Year award in 1988.

WADE BOGGS

Infielder

**Boston
Red
Sox**

◆ ◆ ◆

If anybody was born to be a hitter, it was Wade Boggs. The future American League batting champion was swinging a bat before he could even walk or talk.

Ted Williams, one of the greatest hitters of all time, called Wade "The Natural." During a game telecast in Boston, Ted was shown a picture of Wade batting when he was 18 months old. "I don't know who this guy is," Williams said. "But he's got the perfect swing."

Most major league stars begin their baseball careers when they reach little league age. Wade couldn't wait.

He was already an outstanding hitter before other kids his age even knew what a baseball was. His lessons started with a plastic bat and a whiffle ball about the time he learned to walk.

His father, Win Boggs, tossed the ball while Wade swung the tiny bat. First, he threw the ball down the middle until Wade got used to hitting it.

When Wade could hit the whiffle ball consistently, his dad switched to tennis balls. He also started moving the pitches around—outside, inside, high and low.

By the time Wade was 3 years old, he could adjust to the pitch. That's when his dad used a real baseball and held regular batting practice.

Wade wanted to learn everything about baseball. He watched entire games on television. Afterwards, he ran outside to practice what he had seen. Wade put down pieces of cardboard for bases and pretended to hit the ball and then ran the bases.

"I recognized at an early age Wade had very good hand-eye coordination," his dad said. "That's one reason he became such a great hitter. I never had to teach him much either. It all came naturally."

"I started [organized baseball] when I was 5 years old in Tampa, Florida, and played against kids who were 11 and 12," Wade said. "My father wanted me to play against older kids. It made me develop my ability a lot faster and it got me used to tough competition early."

But there was one time in little league when Wade's incredible natural hitting ability didn't count.

"My very last game in little league was an all-star game when I was 11," he said. "That had been a special time in my life and I really wanted it to end with a bang."

Wade's team got only two hits in the game and he had both of them. In the last inning, Wade was due up. Another hit might have given his team a chance to tie or win.

But the manager pulled Wade for a pinch hitter!

"The pinch hitter struck out and we lost 2-0," Wade recalled. "I know I could have gotten another hit, but I was taught not to argue with the manager."

One of the greatest hitters of all time ended his little league career being benched for a pinch hitter.

"That was my biggest disappointment in baseball," Wade said. "But it taught me that it can happen to anybody. It's a lesson that comes in handy in the big leagues. Sometimes even the best get benched."

TIM RAINES

Outfielder

Montreal Expos

◆ ◆ ◆

Tim Raines grew up dreaming about football. Tim was one of the best football players in the history of Seminole High School in Sanford, Florida, and one of the flashiest runners in the Southeast.

He led his team to a championship his senior year. His team lost only one game and Tim was offered a college football scholarship. "I was going to be another O.J. Simpson," recalled the 1986 National League batting champion. "I really wanted to be a star in the NFL more than I wanted to play baseball. I thought if I couldn't make it in football, I could always go back to baseball."

But one sensational baseball tournament when he was 15 years old turned his life around. Tim played his heart out and won the Most Valuable Player trophy, even though his team never made it to the finals.

"That's when Tim changed his mind about playing football," his dad, Ned Raines, said. "That tournament convinced him he could be a major league baseball star."

Every player in the Florida State Junior League tournament was bigger than Tim who stood only 5 feet 6 inches tall at the time. But his talent stood head and shoulders above them all.

Tim pitched the first game. He struck out 16 and gave up only two hits. In the second game, he caught and threw out three runners trying to steal second.

But it was his bat that really made the

sparks fly. Tim went 5-for-5 with four home runs. He was intentionally walked twice. After his last walk, the next batter struck out. That ended the game and Tim's team lost.

"I think I could have hit another home run if they hadn't walked me," Tim said.

Even though his team didn't reach the finals, Tim was still named the Most Valuable Player in the tournament. His life changed completely. He loved both sports, but he knew he would have to pick just one. His size might keep him out of the NFL, but there was nothing to stop him from becoming a baseball superstar. The MVP award told him that.

For his new hero, Tim picked Joe Mor-gan, the 5-foot, 7-inch former Cincinnati Reds star.

From then on, Tim concentrated on his baseball career. But once in a while, he still dreams about scoring the winning touchdown in the Super Bowl.

"Sometimes the football player in me still wonders what would have happened if I had picked football," Tim admitted. "But I made the right choice. After that tournament, I decided to make the best of my opportunity.

"For every little guy like me who makes it to the big leagues, there are a thousand who don't. Maybe someday I can be another Joe Morgan for a kid who thinks he's too small to play with the big guys."

ANDY VAN SLYKE

Outfielder

Pittsburgh Pirates

◆ ◆ ◆

Andy Van Slyke had to go. He had to go *real* bad, but nobody calls time out and runs off the field just to go to the bathroom. Not even if you're only 9 years old and have been drinking Gatorade all day.

It was a long walk to the restroom at the little league field in New Hartford, New York, where Andy grew up. Even if he had time to get there and back between innings, Andy still hated to miss any of the game. Usually, he could wait until after the game when the whole team made a mad dash for the restroom.

But today was not one of those days.

It was a long, boring game with lots of walks and long pauses between pitches.

Andy was in right field where there wasn't much action so he had plenty of time to think about how bad he had to go. The more he thought about it, the worse it got.

"You know how some of those games get in little league," said the All-Star outfielder and Gold Glove winner. "Afternoon can turn into night and you're still standing out there."

The inning dragged on and on. Andy bit his lip, crossed and uncrossed his legs, and tried not to squirm too much. Suddenly, the batter hit a line drive to right field. Andy took off after the ball and dove to catch it.

He made a great catch and came up

with the ball in his glove. But Andy had landed on a very full bladder and he also came up with a very wet uniform.

"There I was, standing out there in front of everybody with the front of my pants soaking wet," Andy said. "It was pretty obvious I hadn't landed in a puddle of water because it hadn't been raining.

"For the rest of the inning, I tried to play facing the outfield and with my back toward home plate. Fortunately, there weren't any more hits or else I would never have seen the ball."

When the inning ended, Andy tried to run to the bench sideways hoping no one would see the embarrassing wet spot.

"I still heard people laughing at me," Andy said. "When I got to the bench, I grabbed a jug of Gatorade and pretended to accidentally spill it all over me. I wanted my whole uniform to be wet so it would all mix together."

Andy knew what everyone was thinking. He wanted to cry, but he didn't. He wanted to run home, but he didn't. The coach saw Andy's predicament and felt sorry for him. Instead of sending Andy back to the outfield where everyone could see him, the coach had him catch the rest of the game.

With the big mask on and the chest protector dangling to his knees, it was the perfect place for Andy to hide while his uniform dried in the summer sun.

JOE CARTER

Outfielder

Cleveland Indians

◆ ◆ ◆

The 14-year-old kid on the mound was mowing them down.

Batter after batter came to the plate and went down swinging. One strikeout followed another until the young pitcher had recorded an amazing 20 K's.

This wasn't Nolan Ryan or Roger Clemens throwing heat when they were kids. This wasn't even a regular pitcher. This strikeout king was Joe Carter. He pitched a perfect game—and gave it to his Dad as a Father's Day present.

Joe had been looking for a special Father's Day gift for several weeks. He decided that the perfect present to give his dad would be a perfect game.

What made the game extra special was that it was the only game his dad ever coached when Joe was playing. The regular coach was gone that day and Joe's dad filled in.

"I really had my stuff that night for some reason," recalled the Cleveland Indians' slugger. "I just kept striking people out. The only fair ball hit off me was a little dribbler back to the mound. I fielded it and threw the guy out."

Besides striking out almost every batter he faced, Joe also drove in several runs to help win his own game.

Joe played little league baseball around his neighborhood in Oklahoma City. But when he got older, Joe knew that he would have to face tougher competition in advanced leagues if he wanted to improve his baseball skills.

The best competition around was up in Edmond, Oklahoma. He told his dad, Joe Sr., that's where he wanted to play American Legion baseball. Even though it meant a long drive back and forth for practice and the games, his dad agreed to take him and encouraged him to play against the older kids.

Joe Sr. knew his son had the makings of a major league star. He wanted to give him a chance to make it to the bigs, so he didn't mind all the extra driving at night after work. Joe proved he had talent and became a star in Edmond.

"Driving back and forth to the games were special times for me and my dad," Joe said. "Having him there as my coach when I pitched that perfect game was probably the proudest moment of my life. I wanted to give him something extra special for all the things he'd done for me."

BRETT BUTLER

Brett Butler had two strikes against him as a little league catcher. He was small. And he was left-handed.

Buried under all that catcher's gear, Brett looked like a Munchkin in a suit of armor behind the plate. He was so little the umpires were always tripping over him. And when he fired the ball back to the mound, right-handed hitters had to duck or risk getting beaned.

"I was really itty-bitty," said Brett, the San Francisco Giants' hard-hitting center fielder. "What made it really comical to watch was that our star pitcher, John Higgenback, just towered over me. John was six feet tall by the time he was 12 years old. As a freshman in high school, I was only five feet tall and weighed 89 pounds, so imagine how tiny I was in little league."

From the time he started in little league in Fremont, California, Brett's goal was to make it to the big leagues—as a southpaw catcher!

"Because I was so small, I knew I had to attract attention some way," Brett said. "I heard that only a few lefties had ever been major league catchers. I decided that would be my way of standing out."

Brett's little league coaches at first tried to discourage him. They told him that he was too small and that lefties didn't make good catchers. But Brett had a special talent his teammates lacked.

"John threw really hard and, for some reason, I was the only one on the team who could catch him," Brett said. "So whenever John pitched, the coaches had to let me catch."

But it wasn't easy. Brett had to use a regular right-handed catcher's mitt. And the extra padding he put in it to handle John's fast ball made the mitt even more awkward for him. Some of John's pitches were so hard they knocked the ill-fitting mitt off Brett's hand.

"Other catchers chased wild pitches, but I was always running to the backstop to get my catcher's mitt," Brett said. "That usually got a big laugh from the crowd. Finally, my dad found a left-handed mitt somewhere."

The mitt wasn't Brett's only equipment problem. Because he was so small, all his uniforms had to be shortened so he wouldn't get lost in them. The catcher's chest protector dragged on the ground when he stood up and, when he crouched, the shin guards nearly touched his chin.

"When I wore the mask, it felt like I was wearing a bucket with eye holes," Brett said. "And I was always tripping over the chest protector and falling down when I had to go after a foul ball. The size of the equipment just overwhelmed me."

But Brett's size wasn't a drawback when his friend, John, was on the mound. Together, they recorded six no-hitters in their career as battery-mates.

"John threw so hard that kids were afraid of him," Brett said. "That made it easier for me. Sometimes it was just like the two of us playing catch out there. I loved it. Being such a little catcher got me the attention I wanted and gave me the confidence to believe I really could make it to the big leagues."

BILL RIPKEN

Infielder
_____
**Baltimore
Orioles**

◆ ◆ ◆

The tape ball games in the backyard lasted for hours. It was Bill Ripken and his brother, Cal Jr.—one on one—playing a baseball game they invented using a wad of adhesive tape as the ball and a sawed-off broom handle for a bat.

"I don't think either of us ever played harder or wanted to win more than we did in those tape ball games," recalled Bill, the Baltimore Orioles' slick-fielding infielder.

"Cal was bigger, four years older, and more talented than I was, so he always won. Always! I'd get so frustrated, I'd start throwing harder and harder. But he just hit the ball farther and farther. Then I'd start hitting him with the tape ball and that usually ended the game."

For Cal, tape ball was the way to show his kid brother who was the best.

"I was a bad winner," recalled Cal, the American League's MVP in 1983. "I'd gloat and brag about how badly I beat Bill, just to get under his skin. I didn't play for fun. I played to win, especially against my brother."

The tape ball games started when Bill was 8 years old and Cal Jr. was 12. They were living in Asheville, North Carolina, where their dad, Cal Sr., was manager of the Orioles' AA minor league club. There was always plenty of athletic tape around the house or at the stadium where the boys spent a lot of time with their dad. They would wad the tape till they had something about the size of a Ping-Pong ball and use a broomstick or a rolled up baseball program for a bat.

The house they lived in for three years had a circular backyard surrounded by a low stone fence. For a boy with imagination, it looked to Bill like a miniature baseball stadium.

During games, any tape ball hit over the wall was a home run. A ground ball that got by the pitcher meant there was a runner on base. If the ball was caught, it was an out. There was no base running allowed and a folding chair behind home plate was the "umpire." If a pitched ball hit any part of the chair, it was an automatic strike.

Bill's dad said the games helped the boys learn the skills they use today in the majors. "Tape ball was great for developing hand-eye coordination and bat speed," he said. "The boys used a small bat and since the ball never went straight when they threw it, it was tough to hit. Besides, they were pitching from close range and throwing hard, which made it more difficult to hit the ball."

"We didn't think of tape ball as a training ground for the big leagues," Bill said. "We were just kids having fun."

Even now, during long rain delays in the big leagues, the Ripkens like to play tape ball in the clubhouse. Sometimes, other players ask to join in the game, but Bill and Cal Jr. prefer to play the way they did as kids—just the two of them. One on one.

TODD WORRELL

The first time Todd Worrell ever went to bat in a little league game, he was hit on the head with the very first pitch thrown to him. Todd spent the next four years in little league struggling to overcome his fear of another beaning.

"It was the worst thing that could happen to a kid," Todd said. "I know it prevented me from developing into a better hitter."

Todd, the National League Rookie of the Year in 1986, tried out for baseball in his hometown of Arcadia, California, when he was 9 years old. His talent was so obvious that he was assigned to a team of 12-year-olds in a little league known as the "majors."

"There was a lot of talk about me making the 'majors' when I was only 9, but I was in over my head," Todd said. "The first pitch I ever saw in organized baseball hit me on the back of the head. I saw it coming and luckily turned away, but it still hit me hard enough to dent the helmet."

Todd was knocked to the ground, but shook off the frightening blow and trotted to first base. But he couldn't shake off the fear that it would happen again.

"Most 9-year-olds are hesitant and a little afraid of the ball anyway, and getting hit on the head with the first pitch really disturbed me," Todd said. "I knew the 12-year-old pitcher. He didn't like it because a 9-year-old kid had made the 'majors' and was getting a lot of publicity for it. I heard later that he beaned me deliberately. Knowing someone did it on purpose was almost as hard to overcome as the fear of getting hit again."

During the next four years, Todd was terrified of every pitch. It was a struggle just to pick up a bat and walk to the plate. Todd stood as far back in the batter's box as he could and hoped for a walk so he wouldn't even have to swing at the ball.

But Todd didn't quit. He kept fighting against the fear of getting hit again whenever he took his turn at the plate.

"It didn't change overnight," Todd said. "I worked hard and one thing that kept me going was my father's encouragement. He was very gentle about it and reminded me that getting hit like that was a freak thing that probably would never happen again. But he insisted that I keep trying, for my own good."

Todd came from a deeply religious family who prayed with him before each game to help him overcome his fear. His mother, Donna Worrell, said that Todd recited a favorite psalm before each at-bat.

"It gave him inner peace," Mrs. Worrell recalled. "And that was the strength he needed to keep trying and not be afraid."

Todd eventually conquered his fear, but the memory of being hit on the head is still fresh in his mind. "That's why I'm so concerned about hitting batters today when I pitch in the major leagues," Todd said. "I remember what it was like to be on the receiving end. It was the most devastating thing that happened to me in little league."

HAROLD REYNOLDS

Infielder
Seattle Mariners
◆ ◆ ◆

The indoor batting cage at the Oregon State University Coliseum was just too tempting to pass up. Even the locked doors of the Coliseum and the chance of getting caught didn't stop Harold Reynolds from sneaking in and taking batting practice in the cage at night.

Harold, the Seattle Mariners' only two-time All-Star, grew up in Corvallis, Oregon, just across the street from the university campus. For Harold, whose heart was set on a major league career, the batting cage was the pot of gold at the end of the rainbow.

The university baseball team used the cage when the weather wasn't nice enough to practice outdoors. But Harold and some of his little league teammates used it every chance they got—which usually was at night when the Coliseum was supposed to be closed.

"I won't say how we did it, but we found

a way to get inside, turn on the lights, and work out in the cage," Harold said. "Most of the time, we got caught by security guards. They would chase us out, but as soon as they left, we'd sneak back in, turn on the lights again, and take more batting practice. That's how I learned to hit."

But there were times when the guards ran out of patience with the baseball-hungry kids and called their parents. Harold's mother, Lettie Reynolds, always left whatever she was doing and came to take Harold home.

Harold credits his mom for steering him away from more serious trouble during his Coliseum adventures. He says she was always there to encourage his dream of becoming a major league ballplayer.

Mrs. Reynolds was Harold's biggest fan and attended every one of his games from little league all the way through high school. As a single parent raising a large family, she felt it was her duty to support Harold and give him every opportunity to develop his baseball talents.

Even when he was too young to play with his older brothers in backyard whiffle ball games, Mrs. Reynolds insisted that they include him. Until he was old enough to play, Harold was the official scorer and unofficial foul ball chaser for those games.

Mrs. Reynolds showed her greatest support for her son during a crucial loss when Harold was a junior in high school. His team was expected to go all the way to the state championship, but it lost in the last inning of a quarterfinal game.

"I was in center field and there was a runner on second with the score tied in the bottom of the seventh inning," Harold said. "The batter got a clean hit into the gap in right center. I tried, but there was no way to make the play."

Harold chased down the ball. He made a tremendous throw to home plate, but the winning run still scored.

"For a kid that age, it was like life was over," Harold recalled. "I blamed myself for the loss. I walked around out there in center field, crying and throwing my glove. Suddenly, I felt an arm around my shoulder. It was my mother. I said, 'Oh, Mom! What are you doing out here?'"

His mother had seen how upset Harold was over losing the big game. So she left her seat in the stands and went to console him.

"You know how guys put on a big macho front in high school," Harold said. "The last thing I wanted was for my mom to come out there in front of everybody. But she knew how important baseball was to me. Coming out there showed how much she cared and how she was always there to support and encourage me.

"I know that if the same thing happened in an important game today in the Kingdome [home of the Mariners], she would do the same thing. And I would be proud if she did."

DENNIS RASMUSSEN

Pitcher

San Diego Padres

◆ ◆ ◆

The doctors who saw Dennis Rasmussen right after his bicycle accident said he would lose his left foot and never walk again. Dennis's dream of playing baseball in the major leagues was crushed.

But the big left-handed pitcher for the San Diego Padres proved the doctors wrong. Through sheer courage and determination, Dennis made a dramatic recovery and saw his dreams come true.

From the time he started playing in little league, Dennis, who was always a super athlete, had his heart set on a big league career. That dream almost ended tragically on September 3, 1973, just one week before Dennis, then 14, was to start his freshman year in high school. He and his dad were riding their bicycles near their home in San Clemente, California, when Dennis was sideswiped by a speeding car. The collision nearly tore his left foot off. The only thing holding it on was his Achilles tendon.

At the hospital, the doctors wanted to amputate his foot. But Dennis and his parents begged them to save it. After five hours in surgery, the surgeons successfully reattached Dennis's foot. But he was told he would never walk again, and that he wouldn't be able to participate in sports. "I couldn't accept that," Dennis recalled. "I had a lot against me, but I knew I could come back. I wanted to play baseball so bad I refused to give up."

Dennis had several more operations and painful skin grafts on his ankle. He spent months in a variety of casts. With his mom and dad holding him up on each side, he learned to walk all over again. Gradually, he improved, but his left leg was now half an inch shorter than his right. Still, he worked out every day.

In March, Dennis miraculously walked onto the court to play the last 45 seconds of the final junior varsity basketball game of the season. The hundreds of people packed into the gym gave him a standing ovation. "I think every person there was in tears," said Barbara Rasmussen, Dennis's proud mother.

But the ankle was still too weak for baseball. And the skin grafts were too delicate to withstand sliding into the bases. Dennis sat out that summer, but he used the time to learn a new pitching motion. Because his push-off leg was now shorter than the other, Dennis had to compensate and learn to throw differently.

"I learned to do little things that reduced the pain and stress on the ankle when I threw," Dennis said. "It meant changing some of the mechanics."

The pain and swelling in his ankle prevented Dennis from running too much. To keep in condition, he started pedaling a stationary bicycle for hours each day. After pitching, he iced down both his arm and his ankle to ease the soreness. Both are habits he practices in the major leagues today.

Meanwhile, his family moved from California to Boise, Idaho. When Dennis finally walked to the mound to pitch his first game since the accident, only the coach and a few teammates realized what a tremendous accomplishment it was. But Dennis and his family knew. They remembered the slow, painful rehabilitation and the determination that it took for Dennis to return to baseball. That year, Dennis not only pitched again, but he also made all-state in basketball, tennis—and baseball!

"When I came out of surgery after the accident and still had my foot, I knew I would play baseball again," Dennis said. "The doctors told me I couldn't, but nothing was going to stop me from making it to the major leagues."

MARK GUBICZA

Instead of battling other gangs in the streets to prove who was toughest, Mark Gubicza fought opponents in a different way—on the baseball diamond.

"Every year it was like a turf war out there," said Gubicza, a 20-game winner for the Kansas City Royals in 1988. "We never actually fought on the field. But we had the reputation of being the toughest team around. We played hard to win, because if you were on the winning team, you were king of the neighborhood."

From the time Mark first picked up a baseball, he was an outstanding player. In his first year in Little League, Mark was only 8 years old, playing against 10-year-olds. Yet he didn't make a single error as a shortstop or a pitcher in all 20 games, and ended up leading the league in hitting.

In the Roxborough section of Philadelphia where Mark grew up, the competition to be the best team in the neighborhood was as hot as any major league pennant race. Mark was only 10 years old when he learned firsthand just how fierce that competition could be. That was the year he had to battle not only the other teams on the field, but also their angry parents in the stands.

By then, Mark had grown to 5 feet, 3 inches tall and weighed 110 pounds. Besides being much bigger than the other kids, he dominated them on the field.

Whenever Mark played that summer, the parents from the other teams tried to force him off the field. They booed, cussed, and yelled at him, claiming he was too old. Sometimes they demanded to see his birth certificate before they would allow their sons to play against him.

Mark's dad, Tony Gubicza, said the parents hassled Mark because they wanted their own sons' teams to be the best in the neighborhood. He still remembers how tough it was on his son to take all the criticism and keep on playing.

One day, Mark was on the bench crying because he didn't understand why all those adults were screaming at him. So he went into the stands where his father was sitting and asked, "Dad, what am I supposed to do?" His father told him, "Mark, they're trying to rattle you and make you lose. Just stay within yourself and go out and play ball. You can't help it because you're bigger and better than the other kids."

Today, Mark's father says he was especially proud of his son because he learned how to handle a difficult situation. Mark also learned self control and refused to let those mean parents run him out of baseball.

"All that trouble made me more competitive," said Mark. "I still want to win just as bad as I did as a kid. Back then, nobody wanted to go home with a clean uniform. It meant that maybe you weren't playing tough enough."

Now that he's a major league pitcher, Mark Gubicza doesn't have much opportunity to get his uniform dirty. "Sometimes," he said with a grin, "I'll dive for a ball when I really don't have to—just to get dirty."

JIM SUNDBERG

Catcher

Texas Rangers

◆ ◆ ◆

The only time Jim Sundberg ever hit three home runs in one game was when he was 10 years old. And he did it using a bat he didn't know was illegal.

The bat was a Nellie Fox model that was famous for its big, fat handle. The first time Jim saw it at the sporting goods store, he fell in love with it even though the bat was almost as big as he was. He saved his money until he had the $4.10 to buy it.

His dad couldn't talk him out of it.

"It was even uncomfortable for *me* to hold," his dad, Howard Sundberg, said. "Jim could hardly get his hands around it, but he wanted that bat more than anything else."

The first night he used it in a league game at his home in Galesburg, Illinois, everybody laughed at the sight of the little kid lugging the fat bat to the plate. Jim wasn't laughing. During practice, he had hit everything the coach threw at him.

"I was really proud of that bat," recalled Jim, one of baseball's best fielding catchers. "When people started yelling about how I'd never get that big piece of lumber off my shoulder, it really hurt my feelings."

Nobody laughed very long. With the first swing, Jim lined a shot off the center field wall for an inside-the-park home run.

But Jim and his Nellie Fox model

weren't finished. The second time up, he socked another homer over the fence.

When Jim came to bat for the third time and belted another pitch out of sight, the opposing team's manager stormed out on the field howling that Jim was using an illegal bat. The umpire grabbed the bat and told Jim he couldn't use it anymore.

Jim's dad and his coach checked the rules. The only thing they could find wrong with the bat was that it was too fat. Howard Sundberg took the bat to his workshop and trimmed it down.

During the next game, Jim stepped up to the plate with his Nellie Fox bat. The umpire and the opposing manager were waiting for him. They said the bat was still illegal and Jim couldn't use it. Jim's dad argued that he had fixed the bat so Jim should be allowed to hit with it.

"They still wouldn't let Jim use it, but they wouldn't tell him why," his dad said. "Jim didn't understand. He didn't think it was fair since we had made the bat legal. But they wouldn't listen. They just kept saying it was an illegal bat and he couldn't use it."

That year Jim swatted nine home runs, including the three he hit with his illegal bat. The next season he hit only two round-trippers.

"I never hit three home runs in one game again," Jim said. "I could sure use that bat today."

LLOYD MOSEBY

Outfielder

Toronto Blue Jays

♦ ♦ ♦

When Lloyd Moseby tried out for little league baseball for the first time in 1971, he was cut from the squad. The disappointed 11-year-old had to settle for being the bat boy for his friends who made the team.

When tryouts were held the next year, Lloyd tried again. And, for the second year in a row, he didn't make the cut. Coach Jessie Wyatt felt sorry for the disappointed kid and asked him to return as the team's bat boy.

"The first time was bad enough, but the second year, when I was 12 years old, it was really embarrassing," recalled the Toronto Blue Jays' slugger and all-time team leader in extra base hits. "I grew up in Oakland, California, where everybody wanted to play baseball. All my friends made the team, but the closest I could get was bat boy."

For two years, Lloyd went through the embarrassment of picking up the bats and lugging the equipment for his friends. He had to sit on the bench and watch his buddies having fun playing baseball. And because he was just the bat boy, Lloyd wasn't issued a uniform like his friends who made the team. He had to wear street clothes to the games.

Lloyd wanted to play first base, but he had trouble fielding ground balls. During the tryouts, everything hit to him seemed to roll between his legs.

He also had problems making the play at first. More often than not, his feet got tangled up with the bag and he ended up in a heap on the ground. And Lloyd was just as bad at hitting as he was at fielding. He didn't hit the ball once during the batting tryouts.

"I wasn't just a bad player," Lloyd said. "I was a *terrible* player!"

After his second season as a bat boy

ended, Lloyd realized he had only one more chance to play little league baseball. He was determined to make the team on the third try. During the off-season, he worked hard at hitting and fielding. While the other kids were playing football or basketball, Lloyd was throwing and hitting the baseball.

When tryouts rolled around again, Lloyd was ready.

He went to Coach Wyatt and said: "You're not going to cut me this year."

"I told him, 'You're going to have to show me,'" Coach Wyatt recalled. "And he sure did! Lloyd was never a hitter before, but when he tried out the third time, he hit the ball out of the park during batting practice and onto the roofs of the houses across the street."

Instead of first base, Lloyd tried out for catcher and made the squad. Lloyd's powerful bat, and his enthusiasm over finally making the team, inspired his teammates. They went undefeated that season, winning 32 games and the league championship.

"The peer pressure just got to Lloyd," Wyatt said. "He couldn't stand being a bat boy again for all his friends, so he really worked hard and made the team."

For Lloyd, it was a lesson in perseverance. "There was tremendous pain in getting cut twice," Lloyd said. "It would have been easy to just quit and forget about baseball altogether, but I never gave up. The disappointment just made me work harder."

ANDY McGAFFIGAN

When Andy McGaffigan started pitching as an 11-year-old, his arm was so powerful and his control was so wild that batters trembled with fear and umpires ducked on nearly every pitch.

Andy's arm strength amazed everyone who saw him throw. But not even Andy knew where the ball was going when he released it. He wore out catchers who had to chase after his wild pitches. His early appearances on the mound were limited to a few innings because of all the batters he hit and the walks he gave up.

But Andy worked hard and, along with help from an understanding coach, he developed into one of the best little league pitchers in West Palm Beach, Florida.

No one paid much attention to Andy the first time he went out for little league practice. He had never played baseball before.

"Andy started later than the rest of my team," Coach Robert Gero recalled. "The others already knew how to hit, throw, and field fairly well. Andy couldn't do any of those things, but he did have a cannon for an arm. He was incredibly strong. He was also incredibly wild."

Andy, now the Montreal Expos' fire-balling right-handed pitcher, didn't see much action at first. When he did play, Coach Gero usually stuck him in center field late in the game. It was on a long fly ball to center that Andy first showed off his powerful arm. The ball bounced past him and rolled all the way to the fence. Andy chased it down while the batter sprinted around the bases for what looked like an inside-the-park homer. But Andy retrieved the ball, turned, and threw it home on the fly to nail the runner.

"We stood there with our mouths open," Gero said. "That ball was no more than six feet off the ground all the way to home plate. That's when I decided to make Andy a pitcher."

But Andy knew even less about pitching than about playing center field. He didn't know how to hold the ball, how to stride, or how to throw from the mound. Gero taught Andy the fundamentals and made him repeat the movements over and over.

After Andy started pitching, opposing players quickly learned to fear him. "He hit enough of them that nobody wanted to face him," Gero said. "You'd see kids going up to bat with tears in their eyes. Even the umpires were afraid of him. They wore those big, outside chest protectors and Andy was constantly bouncing balls off them. You'd think they invented the backstop just for him. Andy sure gave it a workout with his wild pitches."

But Andy began to tame his wildness. He begged the coaches to stay after practice and help him. If he had no one to throw to, Andy worked by himself on his moves. He threw at the backstop to an imaginary strike zone.

That first year, Andy's team, Communication Workers of America (CWA), went 3-19 for the season. The last game of the season, CWA played the league's top team which was going into the championship playoffs with a 19-2 record.

Andy played most of the game in center field, but late in the game, with CWA leading by one run, Andy got the chance to show his new-found control. He went in to pitch—and didn't give up a single run. CWA won that game and Gero discovered a powerful new pitching star. The next year, with Andy pitching full time, his team did a complete about-face, racking up 19 wins against only 3 losses.

CARNEY LANSFORD

Infielder

Oakland Athletics

♦ ♦ ♦

The pain was enough to make a tough kid cry, but Carney Lansford wasn't going to let a little thing like a broken wrist keep him out of the championship game of the 1969 Little League World Series.

"I didn't care how bad I was hurting," Carney said. "Very few kids get to play in the finals of the Little League World Series and I wasn't going to miss that once-in-a-lifetime opportunity. It was the climax of my Little league career."

Carney, then 12 years old, had broken his right wrist two days before when he was hit by a pitched ball in the semifinal game. The injury ruined the game plan that called for Carney to pitch in the championship game. But he begged the

doctor to remove the cast on his right wrist so he could do something to help his Briarwood teammates from Santa Clara, California.

Briarwood was to play the powerful team from Taipei, Taiwan. Carney's coach had devised a secret strategy that he hoped would give his team an edge over the Taiwanese who were appearing in their first Little League World Series.

"I was one of the two best pitchers on our team," recalled Carney, the Oakland Athletics' hitting star. "The other kid threw hard fast balls and I had a real good curve ball. When we knew we would be in the finals, our coach announced that the other guy would pitch.

"When the Taiwan coach heard that, he

started throwing batting practice from half the distance between the mound and home plate so his kids would get used to seeing a fast ball coming. When the game started, I was supposed to go in with my curve ball and catch them off guard."

That plan fell through when Carney was unable to duck away from a high, hard pitch that hit him on the right wrist and broke a bone.

"There was no way I could pitch," Carney said. "But I knew I could still help out at some other position. I pleaded with the doctor to take the cast off so I could play. He refused to do it without my parents' permission."

But Carney's parents couldn't be reached. They were enroute from California to Williamsport, Pennsylvania, for the championship game. For two days,

Carney frantically tried to track them down by phone.

"They showed up at our team complex two hours before game time," Carney said. "They gave their permission and I got the cast off less than an hour before we took the field."

Carney started the game in right field and later was moved to third base. But it was a losing cause. Prepared to face a fast ball pitcher, and with Carney's hard-breaking curve ball out of action, the Taiwanese went on to a 5-0 victory.

"We got only three hits in that game and I had one of them," Carney said. "I was able to contribute something despite my broken wrist, but it wasn't enough. That was probably the toughest loss I've ever had in baseball."

TODD BENZINGER

Infielder

Cincinnati Reds

◆ ◆ ◆

Todd Benzinger was tired of finishing second to the Amelia Rams. He secretly practiced to master the knuckleball —one of the hardest pitches to control. He then used it to ambush his arch rivals during a playoff game.

If it hadn't been for the Rams, Todd's team, the New Richmond (Ohio) Frisches, would have run away with the Knothole League championship every year. The Frisches could beat the Rams in regular season games, but during the playoffs, the Rams always won.

"Our season revolved around those games," Todd said. "Every year we met the Rams in the playoffs, but we always ended up in second place. It drove me crazy."

When he was 9 years old, Todd decided he wasn't going to lose to the Rams anymore. If he couldn't overpower them with his pitches, he'd baffle them with his secret weapon.

"That year, I discovered that my hands were really getting big," Todd recalled. "For the first time, I was able to get some good movement on the ball."

Todd, the Reds' clutch-hitting first sacker, found that he could now grip the ball well enough to throw a knuckleball for the first time. "I watched [Chicago White Sox hurler] Wilbur Wood throw his knuckler on television and I thought it would be a great trick to spring on the Rams," Todd recalled. "I started practicing and soon I could throw a knuckleball with pretty good control. But it was still the wildest looking pitch I'd ever seen."

It was even wilder for the batters who tried to hit it, according to Todd's coach, Tom Warden. If a knuckleball was hard for a kid Todd's age to throw, it was even harder to hit. Players who had never seen the pitch before thought it looked like a fat, jumping bean floating towards the plate.

When Todd faced the Rams the next time, it was during the playoffs of the county championships. Todd kept the knuckler under wraps and waited for just the right time to reveal his big surprise.

The right time came late in the game when the Rams' player who always gave Todd the most trouble was at bat. "The guy was two years older than me and built like a truck," Todd said. "He always hit the ball a long way. I got an 0-and-2 count on him, so I figured the best way to get him out was to be crafty. That's when I threw the knuckleball in a game for the first time."

Todd and his battery-mate didn't use signs, so his catcher had no way of knowing what was coming. He probably couldn't have caught it anyway. Todd's first knuckleball missed the batter, the catcher, and home plate by 30 feet!

"That was really embarrassing," Todd recalled. "But I knew I could throw the pitch, so I came right back with it. The second time, I got it in there. He swung and missed it by 30 feet. I thought he was going to screw himself right into the ground."

Todd got that batter out and went on to beat the Rams, mainly on the strength of his knuckleball that totally baffled the other kids.

"We finally got through the playoffs and made it to the county championships," Todd said. "We didn't win the championship, but that was okay. My greatest thrill was throwing that knuckleball against the Rams and making them look foolish trying to hit it. After all the times they had beaten us, it felt great!"

BUD BLACK

Pitcher
—
Cleveland
Indians

◆ ◆ ◆

Bud Black and his teammates were the underdogs in the Little League district tournament. They weren't expected to win—and they didn't. But they came close —as close as the last inning, the last out, and the last strike before they threw the ball away and lost the game.

Bud was 12 years old and playing on a so-so team in Longview, Washington. No one thought the team would go far, but suddenly Bud and his teammates were playing for the championship in the district finals. A victory meant a trip to California and a step closer to the Little League World Series. Overnight, people were talking about this Cinderella team that just might go all the way.

Like most of the teams they'd faced all season, their opponent in the finals was bigger, better, and more experienced. But Bud and his teammates played their

hearts out. It really looked like they could pull off a miracle and win the game.

"We got to the bottom of the last inning and were ahead by one run," Bud said. "There were two out and two runners on base and we had two strikes on the hitter."

Bud was playing first base. He called timeout and gathered the infield around the mound for one of their "rock piles."

A "rock pile" was their special name for a conference when they needed to talk things over. Their coach, Glova Sweet, used to tell them to get their heads together out there on the mound and make a "rock pile."

"When they got in trouble, I wanted them to figure it out for themselves," Sweet said. "They understood each other better than they did the coaches."

Out at the "rock pile," Bud made sure

82

everybody knew what to do. On any ground ball, go to first for the out. Don't worry about the runners. Just get the out and the game is over.

"We all knew what we had to do," Bud said. "I went back to first base and on the very next pitch, the batter hit a slow roller to second."

Bud covered the bag. He turned to take the easy toss from the second baseman. The Cinderella team had it all but won. Bud could almost read the headlines now. The state championship! The western regionals! Maybe even the Little League World Series!

"There I was standing on the bag with my glove out waiting for the throw," Bud recalled. "I couldn't believe my eyes! Our second baseman picked up the ball and threw it to *third base*! It would have been

OK if he had thrown it right to third. But he threw it way over the third baseman's head.

"Two runs scored and we lost the game by one run."

Bud and his teammates just walked away shaking their heads. The team that beat them went on to represent the state of Washington in the regional finals in California.

"People around Longview still talk about the Cinderella team that blew it," Bud said. "It was my biggest disappointment in baseball. We got out there in our 'rock pile' so we'd know exactly what to do. We had it won. Then 30 seconds later, we lost.

"Yogi Berra was right. It ain't over till it's over."

GLENN WILSON

For Glenn Wilson, his first home run was the most important one of his baseball career. Unfortunately, it didn't count. Glenn was so excited about hitting the four-bagger that he forgot to touch three of those bags on his home run trot.

Glenn, who led the National League in assists by an outfielder for three straight years (1985-87), was 10 years old and already the biggest star in the history of Channelview (Texas) Little League. He developed his natural abilities with the help of his older brother, Johnie, who started coaching him when Glenn was just a toddler. After watching 4-year-old Glenn practice, the coach of a team of 6-year-olds at the Channelview YMCA asked Glenn to join his team. From then on, Glenn's reputation as an outstanding player spread.

As he got older, Glenn had other Little League coaches, but Johnie continued to work with him at home. Sometimes Johnie pushed too hard and Glenn rebelled. That's how Glenn was feeling when he went to bat after making a costly error in the field.

"When I came in from the field after making an error, I saw Johnie leaning against the fence with a disgusted look on his face," Glenn recalled. "He started yelling at me about the error and I yelled back.

"Finally, he told me, 'Why don't you

quiet down and get in there and hit a home run,'" Glenn said. "It bothered me that I had been playing a long time but hadn't hit a homer yet. There wouldn't be a better time than this, so that's exactly what I decided to do."

Johnie had been trying to get Glenn to change his batting stance to put more power into his swing. But when Glenn stepped into the box, he took his old stance on purpose just to show Johnie he didn't need his help.

Glenn belted the first pitch out of the park. It was a powerful blow! Glenn watched in amazement as it soared over the outfield fence and into the parking lot.

"I've hit a lot of home runs since then," Glenn said. "But I've never hit one that felt that good. When I ran around the bases, I remember it felt like I was floating on air. I was so happy."

Glenn crossed the plate and was surrounded by his teammates. Out of the corner of his eye, he spotted Johnie and realized how proud his big brother was of him. There were tears in Johnie's eyes as he cheered for his little brother.

But the celebration came to a quick end. The umpire pushed through the crowd of happy players and motioned that Glenn was out. On his triumphant home run trot, Glenn had failed to touch first base, second base, and third base!

"I really didn't mind too much," Glenn said. "To me, it was still my first home run, even if it didn't count. And I'll never forget how proud my big brother was of me. That was the best part of all."

KEITH MORELAND

**Infielder-
Outfielder**

**Baltimore
Orioles**

◆ ◆ ◆

If Keith Moreland hadn't gotten in trouble at school, he might never have become interested in baseball. And if his fourth grade teacher hadn't taken him to the Astrodome to see the Houston Astros play, he might never have made it to the major leagues.

Keith grew up in Carrollton, Texas, where football was the only sport most kids were interested in. But when he was 11 years old, Keith attended his first professional baseball game. It changed his life forever. The instant Keith walked into the brand new Houston Astrodome and heard the crowd cheering for baseball players and begging for their autographs, he knew that's what he wanted to be.

"It happened just that fast," recalled Keith, the Baltimore Orioles' veteran hit-ter. "I was in complete awe. I went home and told my parents that I was going to be a major league ball player."

Keith got to see the big league game that changed his life because he was a mischievous kid who sometimes got into trouble in school for his fun-loving ways. Soon after little league practice started in the spring, Keith, a fourth grader, was caught cutting up in class and had to stay after school to clean the blackboards as punishment.

He complained to his teacher that he had to go to baseball practice. "I didn't care that much about baseball," Keith recalled. "I just used it as an excuse to get out of detention."

To his surprise, his fourth-grade teacher knew more about baseball than he did. The teacher, Mrs. Dianne Adair, was married to Jimmy Adair, a coach with the Houston Colt .45s, before they became the Astros and moved into the new Astrodome in 1965.

"I was amazed that a woman, and a teacher at that, knew more about sports than I did," Keith said. He started paying attention to major league box scores so he could talk to Mrs. Adair about baseball. Mrs. Adair encouraged Keith's growing interest in baseball. She and her husband took him to an Astros game that summer. Jimmy Adair showed the wide-eyed boy around the clubhouse and introduced him to the players. Keith left clutching an autographed baseball that became his most prized possession.

"I couldn't believe how great those guys played," Keith recalled. "I was used to little league where everyone dropped the ball or struck out all the time. Major league baseball was a whole new world to me and I knew that's what I wanted to do the rest of my life."

Keith went back to Carrollton and, overnight, dedicated himself to a baseball career. Instead of playing little league just to pass the time until football season started, he worked hard to learn how to hit, throw, and field the ball. And because of his new enthusiasm, his little league team turned into a winning team.

"I became known as Carrollton's baseball kid, while all my friends stuck with football," Keith remembered. "All I wanted to do was play baseball. I told everybody I was going to the major leagues. I was only 11 years old, but baseball just totally occupied my life after seeing that Astros game.

"And to think, I wouldn't be in the major leagues today if I hadn't gotten in trouble in fourth grade and had to stay after school."

MIKE PAGLIARULO

Mike Pagliarulo concentrated so hard on watching the ball during his first four Little League games that he forgot to swing the bat.

The first hitting lesson Mike's dad, Charlie Pagliarulo, gave him was to watch the ball from the time it left the pitcher's hand and to "look" it right into the catcher's mitt. Mike followed his dad's instructions so well that he forgot the next most important lesson in batting —hit the ball.

"Pags," the San Diego Padres' spark-plug third sacker, grew up almost in the shadow of Boston's Fenway Park. He played for the Yankees in the South Medford Little League and his first game was against a team called the Red Sox.

His failure to swing the bat in his first Little League game was so upsetting that he threw up afterwards. "I was so nervous that I didn't even make it as far as the ice cream stand after the game," Mike recalled. "After that, I settled down and didn't throw up anymore, but I still didn't swing the bat."

Mike didn't swing at the ball in his three trips to the plate during the second game. He just watched the ball. In the third game, Mike cocked the bat a couple of times, but still didn't swing and went 0 for 3.

By now, his dad, Charlie, was getting worried. He asked Mike what was wrong.

"There wasn't anything wrong," Mike remembered. "I just got so interested in watching the ball all the way in that I forgot to swing."

After another no-swing, no-hit game, Charlie Pagliarulo decided he had taught his son too well. He took Mike to the ballpark the day before the next Little League game and pitched to him. "My orders were to swing at everything he threw no matter where it was," Mike said.

Charlie said that Mike had done a good job of watching the ball. He had learned to tell a good pitch from a bad one. Now, he wanted Mike to develop a smooth swinging motion. As Mike swung away, Charlie coached him on how to hold the bat, how to turn his wrists, and how to shift his weight when he started to swing.

The long day spent in the batting cage paid off. In the next game, Mike came out swinging. The first time up, he got a single. Mike smacked a long double on his second trip to the plate.

"After that first hit, I was on a roll," Mike said. "I quit thinking about watching the ball so much and concentrated on what my dad told me: 'Attack the ball.'

"My father convinced me to go after everything thrown to me. He still tells me to attack the ball. I've got a reputation now for being aggressive at bat and it's because of that Little League experience. I learned how much more fun it was to hit the ball than just to stand there and watch it go by."

JEFFREY LEONARD

<table>
<tr><td>Outfielder</td></tr>
<tr><td>Seattle Mariners</td></tr>
</table>

◆ ◆ ◆

Jeffrey Leonard was known as the "dirt-iest" player on his little league team. Jeffrey wasn't mean and he always played fair. But he wore the dirtiest uniform in little league—because his dad made him do it.

"My father believed that if I had a dirty uniform, it put me in the mood to play hard and aggressive," said Jeffrey, the only player in National League history to hit home runs in four consecutive games in a championship series when he was with the San Francisco Giants.

"During my first year, I played with guys who came to every game in bright, clean uniforms. We played two or three games a week and, after the first week, I put my uniform in the laundry to be washed. My father told me to leave it dirty. He said it made me look mean and rough."

His dad, Wilson Leonard, coached Jeffrey's little league team in Philadelphia. But he taught more than just how to throw and hit. Wilson wanted his players, especially Jeffrey, to develop a winning attitude.

"It was okay to dive for the ball or to slide into the bag even when you didn't have to," Jeffrey recalled. "If my uniform wasn't dirty enough, my father made me get it dirty. He'd tell me to go out and roll around in the dirt until I looked like a real ballplayer."

Jeffrey's father said the kids with dirty uniforms looked like they played harder. "I wanted the other teams to think about that when they saw Jeffrey on the field,"

Wilson said. "He really wasn't rough. He just looked that way. The other players were a little intimidated when they saw him and that gave Jeffrey an edge."

Jeffrey's team, the Falcons, once won a title game because he wasn't afraid to play hard and get dirty. The Falcons were playing their biggest rivals, the Top Cats, for the championship of Fairmount Park little league. The Falcons were trailing by one run in the last inning with one out and Jeffrey on first base.

"Our team had just about given up," Wilson recalled. "The batter hit what looked like a double play ball, but Jeffrey took off for second base like his pants were on fire."

It had rained the night before and the infield was still muddy. That didn't stop Jeffrey. He dove into second base head first and was called safe. It was the first time he had ever slid into second base that way and he came up covered with mud from head to toe.

"That fired up the whole team," Wilson said. "It gave them new life. The next batter got a hit. Jeffrey scored from second base and we went on to win the championship."

The only one who objected to Jeffrey's "dirty" style of playing was his mom. She wouldn't allow the dirty uniform in the house. Jeffrey had to change on the porch before he could come inside.

"Usually, after a few weeks, I couldn't stand it myself," Jeffrey recalled. "My uniform stunk so bad even my dad agreed it needed to go in the laundry. But my mom refused to clean it. If I wanted a clean uniform, I had to wash it myself."

CHRIS BOSIO

Pitcher

Milwaukee Brewers

♦ ♦ ♦

For 9-year-old Chris Bosio, the last inning of his championship little league game had more ups and downs than a roller coaster ride. He went from hero to goat to hero so fast his head was spinning. Fortunately, when the wild ride ended, Chris was a hero.

"I'll never forget that game," recalled the workhorse of the Milwaukee Brewers' pitching staff.

The score was tied going into the seventh inning of the final game of the season in Rochester, Minnesota. "We were the visiting team," Chris said. "When I came to bat in the top of the seventh, there were two out and a runner on base. I was just hoping for a hit that would give us the lead."

Chris got his wish. He also got the pitch he wanted and hit a booming fly ball to deep left field. The runner on base came around to score.

"I was sure I'd hit a home run and, with a two-run lead, we were sure to win the game," Chris recalled. "I tossed the bat toward the dugout and went into my home run trot. But I got too cocky too soon."

Chris was in for the shock of his life. He was tagged out just as he rounded first base!

"At first, I thought the umpire was kidding," Chris said. "Then I really got mad. I was sure I had hit a home run and that the other team had cheated and thrown in an extra ball. I didn't believe they got the ball I hit back to the infield that fast."

But Chris was out—for not paying attention. The left fielder had lost the fly ball in the lights and it had dropped behind him. When Chris didn't see the fielder catch the ball, he assumed it had gone over the fence.

"I really created a scene, yelling and stomping up and down," Chris said. "It was very embarrassing."

Because of his blunder, the side was retired. But at least his team had a slim lead. If they could only hang on, they would win the championship. In the bottom of the seventh, Chris got the chance to redeem himself. The coach moved him from first base to the mound to pitch to the last three batters.

Chris bore down and got the first two batters out on six straight strikes. "Then I made another dumb mistake," he said. "I got overconfident again and walked the next three batters on 12 pitches."

By now, the crowd was going wild. The bases were loaded and Chris was facing the best hitter on the opposing team. Chris's first pitch was a strike. Then he threw three straight balls before running the count to 3-and-2 with a second strike.

His coach called time and walked to the mound. He put his arm around Chris's shoulder and told him, "Just close your eyes and throw it as hard as you can."

The umpire signaled to play ball. The batter stepped into the box. Chris closed his eyes, reared back, and threw the hardest pitch of his young life. "I threw so hard, my cap came off and I fell down," he recalled. "The next thing I knew, I was being mobbed and everyone was going crazy. I'd thrown a called third strike! We had won the game and the championship.

"I was never so glad to see a game end in my life. I finally ended up as a hero. But it taught me that if you don't give 100 percent all the time, you can just as easily be the goat."

GLENN DAVIS

Infielder

Houston Astros

♦ ♦ ♦

As a Little Leaguer, Glenn Davis looked like a miniature version of Babe Ruth when he went to bat. He routinely blasted line drive homers that just barely cleared the top of the outfield fence as they zoomed out of sight. And once, Glenn literally knocked the cover off the ball!

Glenn, the future All-Star slugging first baseman for the Houston Astros, didn't have the look of a power hitter when he started playing in the Highlands Little League in Jacksonville, Florida. He was overweight and slow on his feet. The only thing that looked promising was his smooth, level swing.

Few of the coaches saw much hope for the roly-poly kid, so Glenn was selected low in the Little League draft. He spent most of the first year riding the bench.

But Marvin Arnett, the coach of the Highlands Indians, liked what he saw when Glenn finally did get to bat.

"I traded and got Glenn the second year when he was 10 years old," Arnett said. "The other coaches laughed at me. Glenn was almost obese, so no one thought he could play ball."

But Arnett had spotted Glenn's potential with the bat. He saw that Glenn's extra weight also gave him tremendous upper body strength. With Arnett's coaching, Glenn learned to use that strength to become a hitter of awesome power. The other Little Leaguers who had poked fun at Glenn soon dreaded to see him at the plate. They were terrified of the screaming line drives he hit at them.

"The outfielders automatically backed

up to the fence when Glenn came to the plate," Arnett recalled. "I've never seen a kid hit a ball as hard as he did. The outfield fence was 180 feet from home plate. He was blasting line drives so hard they were hitting the fence and damaging it. Those line drives were scaring the other kids half to death."

Arnett told Glenn to shift his weight to his back foot in the batter's box. The adjustment gave him more of an upswing and, instead of line drives, Glenn started hitting towering home runs that disappeared over the fence. When he was 12 years old, Glenn set a Highlands record with 25 home runs in one season.

As Glenn grew older, his power improved. One of his teammates at University Christian School was Oakland A's pitcher Storm Davis (They are not related, but Glenn lived with Storm's fam-ily during high school.) Storm's father, George Davis, recalled a game when Glenn swung so hard he actually knocked the cover off the ball. "Glenn was 15 years old and he blasted one of those line drives into left center field. As it went over the shortstop's head, the cover came off and the ball started to unravel. It was like a scene right out of *The Natural*. Glenn just crushed that ball."

In another game, Glenn hit a towering homer that traveled too far to measure. The ball not only cleared the outfield fence, it sailed over the roof of the school gym and disappeared.

"We never did find that ball," George Davis said. "It was the most amazing thing I've ever seen. It went so far, it would have gone clear out of the Astrodome if he had hit it today."

In order to publish this book for the start of the 1990 baseball season, it was necessary to finish it by the end of the 1989 season. As a result, it does not reflect any change of teams that a player might have made through a trade or free agency since the completion of the manuscript.

Throughout this book, we use the name Little League when we are referring specifically to teams that play official Little League Baseball. We use the term little league—without the capital letters—when we are referring to any other youth-oriented organized baseball.